PRAISE FOR *LIFE*

C000125975

"Whether in military combat or business, achieving optimal outcomes is all about setting [yourself up] for success by developing the right preparation, plan, and process. Stephen Drum's *Life on the X* provides an excellent and easy-to-follow framework [so you can] prepare for your most important situations."
—John P. Calamos Sr., major, USAFR (ret.); and founder, chairman, and global chief investment officer of Calamos Investments

"Success at the highest levels of professional sports requires incredible focus [and] mental toughness . . . In *Life on the X*, Stephen Drum expertly translates the skills and methods of the most elite performers into simple and easy-to-follow action steps that anyone can use."
—Michael Cuddyer, fifteen-year MLB veteran and two-time All-Star

"*Life on the X* is one of the best books [ever written] on high-stakes readiness. The next time you've got to be at your best, you're going to thank your lucky stars you read this book."
—Michael Port, *New York Times* and *Wall Street Journal* bestselling author of *Steal the Show: From Speeches to Job Interviews to Deal-Closing Pitches, How to Guarantee a Standing Ovation for All the Performances in Your Life*

"When facing challenges and adversity in any facet of your life, your mindset is the pivotal difference between a positive outcome and one you don't desire. Stephen shows you how to gain a critical mental edge by using easy-to-apply, practical skills based in performance psychology to optimize your success!"
—Elizabeth Lombardo, PhD, bestselling author of *Get Out of the Red Zone: Transform Your Stress to Optimize True Success*™

"So much of leadership is about the energy and presence you bring into a room. Being a credible leader means maintaining focus and composure during challenging times when the pressure is on. In *Life on the X*, Stephen Drum provides an excellent framework that is both simple and engaging and will truly prepare you for your next high-stakes leadership moment!"

—Andrew Swinand, CEO of Publicis Groupe Creative
and Production US and of Leo Burnett Group

"Success in life is mostly about showing up to your defining moments and seizing every opportunity because you are poised, confident, and ready to bring your A game. . . . *Life on the X* shows you how to, in my words, do the 'dark work' to shine in the light so you can 'make shift happen'! Stephen's processes will help you dominate your defining moments!"

—Anthony Trucks, former NFL player, speaker,
and creator of the Dark Work Experience

"How to face high-stakes moments at your absolute best—that is exactly what retired SEAL master chief Stephen Drum provides in this clear, concise, and highly practical book. If you are interested in knowing how to prepare for and execute [difficult situations] with confidence—especially when it matters the most—*Life on the X* is a must read!"

—Rich Diviney, commander, Navy SEAL (ret.); and author of
The Attributes: 25 Hidden Drivers of Optimal Performance

"This book highlights one of the most important aspects of leadership: the process of reflecting and learning from past experiences to make better decisions going forward. It takes courage. Thank you, Stephen!"

—Kristen Hadeed, author of *Permission to Screw Up: How
I Learned to Lead by Doing (Almost) Everything Wrong*

"If you want to learn how to do your best when the money is on the line—if you want to learn how to stay focused when the heat is on—then X marks the spot! The book is packed with tips and strategies that you can use in all aspects of your life to enhance your professional and personal success."

—Hendrie Weisinger, PhD, author of *New York Times* bestseller *Performing Under Pressure: The Science of Doing Your Best When It Matters Most*

"Do you want to double the size of your company without sacrificing your personal life? Navy SEAL Stephen Drum opened my eyes to a whole new level of excellence for my company and for me personally. Stephen's book is a road map to thriving as an entrepreneur in a fast-growing company and becoming the best version of yourself as you lead others to do the same.

"Stephen gives a master class on being brilliant in the basics. He teaches the reader how to be focused on [understanding a] situation, anticipating what comes next, and making the very best decision. Master chief Drum has a unique and engaging skill of sharing compelling combat stories. He pulls out one key principle [at a time] and makes it immediately actionable for the reader. Our leadership team has studied and embraced Stephen's [methodology], and we apply [his] wisdom daily. My recommendation: buy a copy of this book for everyone on your team and watch what happens in the next year."

—John Ramstead, president of Alpha Principle, LLC

LIFE ON THE

X

STEPHEN DRUM

MASTER CHIEF, US NAVY SEAL (RET.)

LIFE
ON THE
X

A Navy SEAL's Guide to Meeting Any Challenge with
COURAGE, CONFIDENCE, AND READINESS

DRUM
HOUSE
PUBLISHING

The views expressed in this publication are those of the author
and do not necessarily reflect the official policy or position
of the Department of Defense or the US government.

Some names and identifying details have been changed
to protect the privacy of individuals.

Seven-step rehearsal protocol used courtesy of Heroic Public Speaking.
Quote from Kristen Hadeed used with her permission.
Quote from John Calamos used with his permission.

Published by Drum House Publishing, Lake Bluff, IL
https://stephendrum.com

Edited and designed by Girl Friday Productions
www.girlfridayproductions.com

Cover design: Megan Katsanevakis
Project management: Reshma Kooner
Editorial production: Abi Pollokoff

ISBN (paperback): 979-8-9863045-0-2
ISBN (e-book): 979-8-9863045-1-9

Library of Congress Control Number: 2022922298

CONTENTS

Introduction 1

Part 1: Commit

Chapter 1: Values 15
Chapter 2: Principles 23
Chapter 3: Attributes 28
Chapter 4: Purpose 36
Chapter 5: Character. 44
Chapter 6: Commitment 49

Part 2: Prepare

Chapter 7: Objectives 58
Chapter 8: Be Brilliant on the Basics. 65
Chapter 9: Mental Skills: Manage Energy and Focus. 73
Chapter 10: Mindfulness Training 84

Part 3: Execute

Chapter 11: Rehearsal 93
Chapter 12: Contingencies 101
Chapter 13: Situational Awareness 107
Chapter 14: Agility. 113

Part 4: Reflect

Chapter 15: After-Action Review and Assess 121

Chapter 16: Manage Feedback 128

Chapter 17: Opportunity: A Mindset 134

Chapter 18: Separate Outcome from Execution 139

Planning for Your Next High-Stakes Event 143

About the Author. 149

INTRODUCTION

The heat of the Iraqi sun felt absolutely brutal as I sat on a pile of sandbags on a rooftop in a highly dangerous area of Baghdad. My first Iraq deployment was in the summer of 2004. I had joined the SEAL Teams in 1996 and completed several real-world operations, such as ship boarding and reconnaissance missions, but this deployment would be my first taste of what real combat was like.

I pulled out my laser range finder to gauge the distance to some of the more distant buildings and alleyways across the street from our position before getting behind my sniper rifle and scanning for threats in my scope. Lying prone in front of me was my fellow SEAL sniper who was covering the street to my left. With us on the rooftop were about eight US Army soldiers who were protecting us as we provided overwatch security for a friendly Army patrol that would be moving down the street shortly. I had been out like this several times before, in both day and night, and taken ineffective fire, or rounds that were being fired around our positions but not close enough to really be concerning. This time, however, it felt like we were hanging out there on a rooftop with less cover and more exposure to enemy fire.

On the streets below there was a bit of hustle and bustle going on. It looked typical of a somewhat run-down Middle Eastern neighborhood you might see in the movies. A half-dozen kids below were kicking a soccer ball around, and some men were drinking coffee at a café across the street. A few cars and small trucks passed by. Slowly, though, my teammate and I noticed that things began to get a bit quieter. We observed the kids begin to drift away and the adults get up and go inside. It felt too quiet.

Moments later, rounds began to snap right past my head. Supersonic rifle rounds that travel close emit a loud snap like someone firing a cap gun by your ear. The rounds impacted the wall behind us. More rounds began kicking up puffs of dirt and dust in front of us. Farther back behind us I heard the sound of a belt-fed machine gun and our soldiers yell out as they engaged enemy insurgents moving up on the rooftops. We returned fire, battling targets across the street from us.

The enemy fire began to pick up, and just then my SEAL teammate got up and dove past me, yelling "Grenade!" Somehow an insurgent had gotten close enough to lob a grenade onto our position. The grenade bounced over the ledge and struck my teammate in the forehead before landing almost at my feet. Still sitting on my pile of sandbags, I had just enough time to spot the grenade and turn away as I braced myself. It went off and rocked me! Immediately I felt down my right side for any wounds. Nothing! Between the rounds just missing my head and the grenade going off at my feet, it was a miracle I was not hit. Still, my ears were ringing and I was stunned.

It was in this moment that something very interesting happened. I flashed back to the urban-warfare training we conducted in mock cities in training areas at various locations in the southern US—basics that we trained on. Basics that we practiced over thousands of hours.

Back on the rooftop, I felt fear and the uncertainty of not knowing exactly what to do next. What I did know was that I was in charge of figuring things out and that we were taking heavy fire and could not hold this position. Beneath all the fear and confusion, however, was the knowledge that my teammate and I had been well trained and, because of the intensity and realism of the training, there was a feeling of familiarity. My confidence grew and I brought my focus back to what was next. We were going to suppress the enemy fire, maneuver, and get everyone off the rooftop and home safely.

BACKGROUND: THE PATH TO ELITE

Here's how it works to become an enlisted Navy SEAL. Those interested in the program must first commit to joining the US Navy and selecting a regular Navy job. From there, a candidate can screen for the SEAL program, and if they pass the basic medical and physical training test, they may be picked for a SEAL contract. Upon successful further screening and graduation from Navy basic training, they will be given orders to join an eight-week preparation course before being sent through the initial selection process known as Basic Underwater Demolition/SEAL Training, or BUD/S. Naval officers or prospective officers are given an officer-specific preselection process for assignment to BUD/S. Once at BUD/S, all officers and enlisted undergo the same training.

BUD/S is the grueling six-month initial selection and assessment process for entry into the US Navy's Sea, Air, and Land Teams, or SEAL Teams. This basic training is broken into four parts:

- **Basic Orientation Phase:** Here students are exposed to the organization, standards, graded tests, and some of the torturous physical evolutions at a much lower intensity than in the following phases.
- **First Phase—Conditioning Phase:** In this phase, the trainee is tested on physical and mental endurance and toughness. Timed standards for the four-mile run, obstacle course, and two-mile swim must be met. Trainees are assessed in water competency with evolutions such as the underwater swim, lifesaving, and drownproofing. The candidate's ability to work in a team is assessed through small-boat handling and log PT (physical training). The five-plus-day suffer-fest known as Hell Week is the major milestone in this phase.
- **Second Phase—Dive Phase:** In Dive Phase, students are taught the basics of scuba and closed-circuit oxygen diving. There is a strong focus on academics while the standards for the physical tests are increased. The major milestone here is the pool competency evolution.

- **Third Phase—Land Warfare Phase:** Timed standards for the physical evolutions are again raised. There is a lot packed into the third and final phase. Students are instructed and tested on land navigation, small-arms marksmanship, demolition, and land warfare tactics. The training culminates in the final week with the planning, rehearsal, and execution of full-mission land warfare training scenarios.

BUD/S itself is first and foremost a selection and assessment process. Though the trainees learn very basic diving and combat skills, the primary focus is on assessing the trainees in the various operating environments that SEALs work in. If a sailor successfully completes BUD/S training, there is a final phase of training, SQT, which is SEAL Qualification Training. In SQT, the selection is still ongoing, but the focus is primarily on teaching actual combat skills that will close the gap between the raw basics at BUD/S and the advanced skills they will learn in the SEAL Teams.

The enlisted stats for successfully becoming a qualified SEAL can be difficult to track depending on where you start the tracking process, but it essentially looks like this:

- Several thousand civilians annually meet with a US Navy recruiter to apply for the SEAL program. Of those who apply, approximately 1,500 are given a contract that year.
- About 20 percent of those given a contract successfully complete BUD/S training.
- The six-month SEAL Qualification Training has a graduation rate of about 99 percent.

It is important to note that the selection process is ongoing once a new SEAL arrives at the SEAL command. It is not unusual for a SEAL squadron to lose a few operators during a twelve-month predeployment training cycle due to performance issues.

THE PROBLEM: COMBAT INEFFECTIVENESS IN THE FLEET

In April 2017, the chief of naval personnel conducted a comprehensive review of the training and curriculum at the Recruit Training Command (RTC). This is the US Navy's basic training center, or boot camp. This review was preceded by several events in the Navy fleet that revealed how in several real-world incidents, when our sailors were faced with combat situations, or accidents, they were not responding in an effective way. They were not responding as warfighters, or warriors. These events and the findings of the RTC training review were placed on the backdrop of what many senior leaders feared: potential open-seas naval combat with peer and near-peer competitors, the likes of which hadn't been seen since World War II. Navy leadership's conclusion was that our sailors needed to be tougher—warrior tough.

THE SOLUTION: IDENTIFY QUALITIES OF SUCCESSFUL SEALS AND OTHER HIGH PERFORMERS AND DEVELOP A PROGRAM TO TURN NAVY RECRUITS INTO TOUGH AND CAPABLE WARFIGHTERS

I arrived at US Naval Recruit Training Command in 2015 to run the Dive Motivator Division, which oversees separate training for all US Navy Basic Training (boot camp) recruits that have contracts for SEAL, diver, aviation rescue, EOD, and Special Warfare combatant-craft crewmen programs. It was our division's job to get these candidates ready for the next phase of their selection process upon graduation from boot camp. We did this through specially programmed run-and-swim workouts while also giving them frequent mentoring sessions.

In response to the findings of the review, I was tapped in October 2017 to help create the new Warrior Toughness Program (WTP) for all Navy boot camp recruits (separate from training SEAL candidates), and later, other officer programs. I worked both jobs concurrently before going full-time into the WTP the last couple of years before I retired.

In developing the WTP, I was practically locked in a room with a Navy clinical psychologist and a Navy chaplain and told to figure out how to toughen up our sailors. The admiral in charge of the initiative selected the three of us because he wanted to get after toughness using a mind, body, and soul approach.

A senior-enlisted Navy SEAL such as me ought to know how to train sailors for the fight, but more importantly I would bring credibility to teaching young sailors beyond that which non-warfighting subject matter experts could deliver.

The psychologist was tasked with building mental performance into the program. She began by researching other military programs that had similar goals. She also looked at proven methods and techniques for high-stakes performance in sports psychology and mindfulness training.

Navy chaplains play a very important role for the naval force by meeting the spiritual needs of sailors. Whether that sailor is religious or not, the chaplain is there for counseling and advice. For the Warrior Toughness Program, the chaplain was responsible for the character-development aspect of the program. We need tough sailors, but we also need them to be people of character. Sailors with strong character will be more committed to the fight; they are the ones who can be relied on to make the right decisions in challenging situations without direct supervision.

WHAT IS TOUGHNESS?

It was our job to answer this question. We had to know exactly what *toughness* meant in our context, and we had to be able to describe it very clearly.

When it comes to creating a quality like toughness, many people are familiar or more comfortable with its softer and fuzzier cousin, resilience. In fact, we were often asked by senior military leaders and politicians whether the Warrior Toughness Program was just resiliency training.

When it comes to resilience, much of the general talk and even the definitions refer to recovering from or bouncing back from trauma or hardship. If you are resilient, then you can face hardship and suffer minimal effects from that situation. In fact, every sailor up to that point had to conduct mandatory online resiliency training.

With this program, as well as the term *resilience* in general, much of the focus is on what happens after. More focus needed to be applied to the "left of bang," as we say. It's one thing to recover after a traumatic event, but it is quite another to actually be able to perform during the event.

With Warrior Toughness we wanted to teach that recovery piece; that was part of it, but we needed toughness and performance on the spot, or "on the X," as we say in the Teams. We needed warfighters to do their job and win!

Before we could actually design a program to build Warrior Toughness, we needed to define what that was. We needed the extremes of high performance when sailors were taking fire or trying to save a damaged ship, but we also needed to help them cope with the stresses of military life. The techniques and methods that we wanted to teach them had to serve across the broad spectrum of challenges in their professional *and* personal lives.

DEFINING WARRIOR TOUGHNESS

You would be right to think that being a warfighter is about the precision of battle, and everything that goes with it: weapons training, tactics procedure, and planning. But what civilians fail to appreciate, and what the Warrior Toughness Program addresses, is the whole person. And much of that work is about mental preparation and performance—deciding who you are and what matters, building resilience and commitment, and having the mental fortitude to persevere through it all.

We decided that tough sailors and officers could do three things:

1. Take a hit and keep going.

SEALs are taught early that they are never out of the fight and there is always something they can do to improve their fighting position. In a combat situation our Navy sailors may become wounded. They may be shocked at what they see. They may witness their friends die or become wounded, but they must get back in the fight. The fate of an entire ship may lie in the hands of a few sailors and their ability to do their job.

Military folks also face the same challenges as any other professional or person in general may face. They may suffer loss of loved ones, or loss of a relationship. They may get passed over for that expected promotion they felt was justly deserved.

Taking hits in life and moving on requires resilience, but taking a hit in a fight or in the face of adversity and staying in that fight and winning requires more than a typical approach to resilience. It requires certain attributes and skills that anyone can learn or further develop.

2. Perform under pressure.

There is no greater pressure than the life-and-death situation of combat or a combat-like situation such as firefighting on a ship. If fear is gripping us too tightly, then we cannot be in the driver's seat and stay focused and engaged. We cannot think critically and make good decisions. We cannot be effective.

Though it may not be life-or-death, there are plenty of other times in a sailor's life when emotions and conditions conspire to derail them from being present, focused, and able to give their best. The effect of military life on the family is a significant source of pressure. A sailor that can lead their family through high levels of stress based on deployments or short-notice relocations is a healthier and more effective sailor at work.

No matter what the pressure is in a sailor's professional or personal life, they must be able to respond with the right action, choice, or behavior. They must respond and not react blindly or give in to negative emotional impacts.

3. Deal with the "day in, day out" grind.

A typical six-month deployment can be a significant grind to the individual sailor and the unit as a whole. Operational tempo may be very high, which causes extreme physical and mental fatigue, with these becoming more intense toward the end of deployment.

Conversely, there are deployments that are very boring by comparison. In situations like this it is easy for a sailor to lose focus, get distracted, and ultimately become complacent.

A SEAL may find themselves weary and maybe becoming a little careless during the tail end of a high-tempo deployment. There are many jobs in the Navy that can be quite monotonous most of the time. A sailor may watch a radar screen for hours where 99 percent of the time nothing happens, but when it does, many people will be hurt or killed if that sailor becomes disengaged from their job.

Part of being tough is having the training and discipline to maintain focus in the face of extreme fatigue or monotony.

We knew that for the WTP to be effective, it had to help our young sailors at boot camp and also grow into a broad, long-lasting program.

RESULTS

Between January and August 2018, one feasibility pilot and three research pilots were conducted in order to determine program effectiveness and proof of concept.

While the Navy has not yet officially released the data from the study and control groups at press time, the research yielded statistically significant outcomes that the program was indeed effective in the areas measured. The studies found performance improvements in the areas of physical fitness, swim qualification, and stressful inspections that recruits are tested on. One of the most interesting and unexpected findings of the pilot programs was the increase in "on-time graduation rates." This phrase refers to recruits finishing in the training division that they started boot camp with. Often the pressure and grind of basic training leads recruits to seek comfort by going to medical staff with embellished injury or illness. Getting sailors to graduate on time is a significant benefit to the Navy as it saves money and gets sailors to where they are often desperately needed. With the WTP, the results were fewer sailors seeking medical assistance and thus missing training.

USING WARRIOR TOUGHNESS TO
ENHANCE YOUR PERFORMANCE

In this book, I often to refer to high-stakes moments and situations as being "on the X." The "X" is borrowed from my experience in the military; it's a term from military doctrine that indicates where the objective is. When operators fast-rope out of a helicopter onto the rooftop of the target building, they refer to that as "roping—or landing—on the X." The X is also widely used when the enemy engages or ambushes the team. That spot where the enemy fire is directed is known as the X. In these moments, the typical action or phrase is to "get off the X" and out of the kill zone. In short, the X represents what is often the most critical aspect of the operation or the most dangerous part of the mission. It is also often where the opportunity for success exists, provided that you are well trained and well prepared, and have the mental skills to perform in the clutch when the pressure is on! I am intentional with the use of extreme examples because when we gear our training to the extreme, the easier, routine activities become more seamless.

Your personal safety or financial well-being may not hang in the balance on a daily basis, but are you really maximizing every opportunity that comes your way? Are you executing at a high level professionally? Are you showing up in your relationships and social situations in the way you want or need to? What about your recreational pursuits? A golf game with your friends is not typically high stakes, but we lead richer lives when we work to improve, perform at our best, and enjoy the feeling of personal achievement.

The intent of this book is to develop a complete process that you can use consistently. All of us experience life on the X to some degree. We don't want to just survive on the X, though—we want to thrive. We want to perform at a high level! Performing on the X is about being the warrior, leader, teammate, or parent that you want to be when it matters most. Putting the work in and devoting yourself to a process that enables your success in high-stakes moments is what it takes to get there. It will be worth it!

This book demonstrates how military and civilian leaders learn and use techniques in order to perform in high-stakes moments. In every chapter, you will have an opportunity to apply these techniques to build your own system to perform on the X. You will flesh out some fundamental values, beliefs, and principles that you will align with behaviors and actions to propel you in the right direction when the seas get rough. You will find that some of the principles and techniques overlap. Certain ones are dissected for ease of digestion and will be revisited and reinforced in later chapters.

BECOMING WARRIOR TOUGH TO PERFORM ON THE X

During my twenty-seven years in the military, I've had the privilege to serve with some of the most elite warriors on the planet in some of the most challenging situations. I know a few things to be true when it comes to high-stakes performance:

1. You need a proven process that you can perform consistently as a matter of routine. This process must be comprehensive and driven by intention, purpose, character, and commitment.
2. This process must ensure a focus and discipline regarding preparation and the fundamentals of any task or goal.
3. When the stakes are high and the pressure is on, we must ensure that we stay focused and engaged. Your process needs to consider what happens when things go off script or not according to plan.
4. Finally, when it comes to growth and improvement, we will only realize our full potential when we learn how to draw the right conclusions from our lessons and experience and put them into a deliberate plan to prepare for what's next.

In this book, through stories, techniques, and your own actions, you will develop your own process to perform on the X.

Part 1

COMMIT

REFLECT

PREPARE

EXECUTE

How do you identify your own inner warrior? We all have unique gifts, and the strength of our character shows through our commitment to our own path. In this part of the book, I will take you through elements to determine your path and action steps you can take to support it.

As an example, the following is a story that shows character and commitment tested through a SEAL's journey:

After an initial orientation, BUD/S training is broken into three six-week phases. The first phase is Conditioning Phase, followed by Dive Phase and then Land Warfare Phase.

The hammer, as we say, is brought down immediately in First Phase.

In my particular class we lost more than twenty men in the first four days of First Phase. During this phase, the typical day might start with physical training at 5:00 a.m., followed by a meal across the street. You are not permitted to walk anywhere, so going to and from the dining hall itself equals six miles of running daily. After breakfast there may be a room inspection, where all gear and cleanliness are inspected. You seldom pass a room inspection, but the consequences are another opportunity to get wet and sandy and undoubtedly face some more physical torture.

Following lunch there would typically be some type of pool evolution, where you would train and be tested on skills such as lifesaving or drownproofing. The lifesaving test involves subduing and towing a combative instructor from the middle of the pool back to the wall. For drownproofing, a candidate is tested on their ability to swim and float with their feet and arms tied behind their back. These are very challenging evolutions for many candidates, and often they are dropped from training for repeatedly failing these tests.

After the pool evolution, the class would likely finish up with an obstacle course or conditioning run on the beach, followed by another run to the chow hall. The remaining days of the week would look pretty similar but would plug in different evolutions such as ocean swims, log PT, or small-boat handling. These sound like busy and exhausting days, but they're made much harder by the impromptu "hammer" sessions, as we would call them, where instructors would mete out extra pain and punishment for actual or concocted offenses. For every mistake the class or an individual made, often contrived, there would be a series of physical punishments such as bear crawls or eight-count bodybuilders, a modified version of burpees. In my view, these "hammer" sessions were the icing on the cake in making BUD/S that much harder. The planned evolutions were enough of a grind, but when these sessions were added, you never knew how long they would last, and it definitely added to the cumulative grind of BUD/S training.

It is often said that almost any supremely fit individual can make it through one day of BUD/S training; however, it is the cumulative effect of training that seems never-ending, which causes so many to drop on request, or DOR—the term for voluntary disenrollment, or quitting.

CHAPTER 1

VALUES

This book is about being your best in intense, high-stakes moments and situations. It's about learning to see every situation, no matter how difficult or painful, as an opportunity and a challenge.

It is easy for most of us to be our ideal selves when life is tracking smoothly. When we don't feel pressure, it's easier to be kind and honest, to demonstrate patience. When the topic of values is brought up, many will roll their eyes as they recall Boy Scouts or Sunday school.

During hard times we need consistency in execution and confidence that our actions and behaviors will survive the scrutiny of those we most respect and admire. Did our actions and choices make us proud? Did we act in keeping with the morals, ethics, and performance standards that are expected of us?

If we want our best performance on the X, we must be guided by principled decision-making that is underpinned by the values that are most important to us. These values steady us and drive us to put in the work and be resilient when faced with challenges and setbacks.

WARRIOR TOUGHNESS VALUES

The US Navy has its core values—honor, courage, and commitment—which are taught almost from day one. Below are the paraphrased definitions of the Navy's core values:

Honor. Navy sailors are expected to conduct themselves in the highest manner of honesty, integrity, and ethical behavior in their professional and personal lives. This must be exhibited with superiors, subordinates, and peers alike.

Courage. Navy sailors must have the moral and mental strength to make the best decisions in the best interest of the Navy and our nation without regard to personal consequences.

Commitment. Navy sailors must be invested at the highest levels in moral character and professional competence. They must demand dignity and respect for all people up and down the chain of command, regardless of race, religion, or gender.

When we created the Warrior Toughness Program, we knew that we needed sailors to understand and align their behaviors and personal beliefs with the core values. Not everyone who joins the Navy has values that are consistent with these, and many simply don't know how to align their values and beliefs with the Navy's core values. That was our job.

The problem was that as great as these values are, they are taught in Navy Boot Camp, or basic training, and then little exploration is done beyond that. Honor, courage, and commitment became white noise that many did not take very seriously.

PT: A TEST OF VALUES

I had the opportunity to test my values early in my training. As you might imagine, physical training, or PT, is intense and constant. Often these sessions were especially brutal and seemed punitive in nature. It was often a fine line between hard PT and the straight-up "hammer sessions" that I referred to earlier.

During a hammer session early in First Phase, an instructor was deriding us for some real or imagined transgression the class had committed. We lined up in the sand and were put through a rotation of torturous exercises. We went from mountain climbers to burpees for a seemingly endless amount of time. When our upper bodies were beyond muscle failure, we collapsed on our backs for leg levers, flutter kicks, and other abdominal exercises until we could barely lift our legs off the sand.

As the instructor would walk around harassing the candidates that he deemed were underperforming, he would invariably turn his back on some of us, and the game would begin. When the instructor wasn't looking, many of us would slack off to get a quick break. Though we were in awe of the instructors, we knew they didn't have eyes in the back of their heads. I was among those who cheated and lowered my legs when the instructor wasn't looking. Just then, we heard a voice behind us. "If they could see you now. Your friends and relatives back home. If they could see you cheating and putting in so little effort. What would they think?"

One of the instructors had quietly walked in behind us. I must admit that of course I felt a bit shamed by this, though the instructors likely expected many to cheat at PT when no one was looking (in fact, there is an expression in the Teams: "If you ain't cheating, you ain't trying").

This was a pivotal moment in my character discovery and development. What was most important to me? How did I want to be seen by those who mattered in my life? My teammates, my family? Would I have the strength of character to commit and respond with the right actions and behaviors when things got hard? This would be the start of examining what values, principles, and attributes would not just get me through SEAL training but also allow me to be someone who could be counted on to do the right thing when times were tough.

It was in fact my values that would see me through not just the six months of BUD/S training but a twenty-seven-year career.

HONOR: YOUR VALUES IN THOSE YOU ADMIRE

Cheating on PT exercises in BUD/S is common practice, but it got me to start thinking about integrity and honesty. I wanted to be seen as someone who lived those values while also demanding them from my teammates.

As a kid, my uncle Jack was almost like my second father. He was a retired naval aviator and American Airlines pilot and supported me every step of the way in pursuing my dreams of military service. During high school, he drove me down to Virginia Beach so I could meet some real Navy SEALs to get a taste of what the training and lifestyle would be like.

I joined the US Navy out of high school with the express purpose of being a Navy SEAL. The problem for me, though, was that I was terrible at math and missed the required score to qualify for BUD/S training. Instead of going to SEAL training, I received orders to the naval submarine base in Groton, Connecticut, where I would work pier-side on fast-attack submarines. I don't know what made me feel dumber, my math score or the fact that I believed my recruiter when he said I could get a waiver for the few points I'd missed. It would be two years before I could even apply for BUD/S, and I was discouraged. Uncle Jack encouraged me to retake the military aptitude test for which I needed a higher score and even gave me some money to find a math tutor. I made next to no money as a newly enlisted sailor, so having his help to hire a math tutor was pivotal. I passed the aptitude test and was accepted into BUD/S.

My uncle's support meant everything to me, and had I not given max effort to the BUD/S training, I wouldn't just be letting myself down, I would be letting him down as well. Uncle Jack placed a sizable wager with his retired CIA friend that I would make it through training. He believed in me and was always there to support me. I was very happy to have him at my BUD/S graduation six months later.

Later in basic training (and throughout my career in the Navy), whenever I felt the urge to slack off or let up, I remembered the instructor's words: "if they could see you now"; that moment helped me realize that two of the values that drove me the most were loyalty and reputation. I always felt that sense of duty and obligation to come through for those who put their faith and trust in me. Though peer pressure is often thought of as negative, it is often helpful to have others hold us accountable for acting out our values. When we know others hold us to certain standards, it is easier for us to stick to the right path.

COURAGE: IT COMES IN ALL SIZES

Courage is having the strength and conviction to do the right thing in a difficult situation. Though you may not need to summon courage in life-or-death situations as we do in the military, it is still required at times in daily life. When you are performing on the X, presenting to a leadership team, or giving a talk at a big conference, you will need to draw on your own courage to deliver.

Six Hours in Hell: The Story of a Real-Life Rambo

On May 2, 1968, Staff Sergeant Benavidez was listening to the radio transmissions of another Special Forces team under heavy enemy fire, with men severely wounded and desperately needing immediate extraction. Upon realizing that those in the team were good friends of his, he climbed into a helicopter that was spinning up, ready to take off. He had just enough time to grab a medical aid bag and a bowie knife. After arriving at the landing zone (LZ), he jumped off the helo and ran seventy-five meters through withering fire to his fallen comrades.

For six hours, Benavidez treated the wounded and held off the enemy by directing close air support. After one of the recovery helos crashed at the LZ, he collected the wounded and set up a defensive position around the original helo. Finally, another helicopter was able to land, and one by one, Benavidez made multiple trips to carry the dead and wounded and load them onto the helo. During this process he suffered multiple wounds, fighting the enemy with small-arms fire and hand to hand. Severely wounded, he climbed into the helo after all the others had been loaded.

When they finally landed back at the airfield, his wounds were so grievous that he was written off for dead and was being zipped up in a body bag. With his eyes sealed shut from dried blood, and unable to speak from a broken jaw, he summoned up just enough strength to spit in the doctor's face to indicate that he was alive. He had suffered a total of thirty-seven bullet, shrapnel, and bayonet wounds.

Master Sergeant Benavidez retired in 1974 after twenty-four years of military service, and in 1981, President Reagan awarded him the Congressional Medal of Honor for his actions on May 2, 1968.

Benavidez openly stated that the values most important to him were duty, honor, and country. He was often asked if he would do it all over again. He responded by saying, "There would never be enough paper to print the money, nor enough gold in Fort Knox to pay me to keep from doing it again." It was courage and selflessness that drove him to board the rescue helo armed only with a medical bag and knife.

COMMITMENT: TESTING YOUR VALUES IN WHERE YOU SPEND YOUR TIME AND RESOURCES

Commitment is probably the most important value when it comes to making it through SEAL training. I was fully committed to successfully graduating from SEAL training. To do that, I had to commit to every element of the training, not just when we were cold, wet, and tired. I had to commit to my academic studies, my gear maintenance, and my physical recovery. Above all, though, I had to commit to my teammates, because you don't make it through that training on your own, and doing it with and for your teammates is paramount.

It is essential that we identify the values that give us strength and the ones we may need more investment in. Once we identify these values, we can align them with principles that we act on.

We may think we have certain values or that certain things are highly important to us, but a close examination of where we spend our time and resources will uncover whether those beliefs are accurate or not.

Testing Your Commitment: Can You Commit to Change Weakness into Strength?

Tom, a young man in his late twenties, came to me as a coaching client, initially looking for direction and performance improvement. Tom felt unfulfilled with his current job as a software engineer and wanted to take the leap to computer data science. Though this new role involved a whole new set of complexities and required skills, Tom felt he had everything it took to excel in this field.

But he was discouraged because he could not seem to get past the initial stages when going through multiple job interviews. I asked him how committed he *really* was in landing a job in this field.

Naturally, he seemed a bit taken aback by my question and proceeded to explain the certifications, statistical models, and predictive algorithms he had invested in getting and creating in preparation for the interviews.

As we talked, Tom seemed to be a very intelligent and passionate young man, yet his conversation was fragmented and meandering. His presentation was awkward and unengaging. I had to believe that this came across the same way to any potential interviewer.

I pressed him on his interview and presentation preparation. "How do you prepare for your interviews? Do you role-play or rehearse clear and polished answers to a list of potential interview questions? Do you focus on posture or eye contact during a virtual interview?"

Tom admitted that he did not do any of those things because of how much anxiety it caused in preparing for the interview. It may be easy to criticize Tom's lack of dedication toward action that would lead to what he really wanted, but most of us are like that when it comes to our values.

In my own business, I would pour countless hours into my content and rehearsal for upcoming speaking engagements. If you asked me if I was "all in," or fully committed when it came to my business, I would assuredly say yes! Upon closer examination, you would find that my marketing and outreach practices left much to be desired. Like Tom, I was investing in the values of passion, knowledge, and skill-building, but not necessarily the values I needed to be successful. When working with Tom, we got him to the point where preparation and rehearsal were less overwhelming and stressful. Sometimes we just need a little help with action steps that support our values, leading to successful behaviors.

Tom's passion and thirst for learning needed to be augmented with committed practices.

When I spend hours rehearsing a talk, I am valuing professionalism and reputation. It is essential that I am committed and connected with these values; if I lose my way, it may cost me in my relationships and professional success. So I commit and I prepare to perform on the X.

Action Steps: Naming Your Values

Identify your three Warrior Toughness values—what resonates in your gut as the principles or qualities that most matter to you? If you are struggling to name them, here are some exercises that may help:

1. Identify the warriors you admire. Who in your life has demonstrated values that resonate with you? My uncle Jack was like a second father to me. He taught me the value of friendship, kindness, poise, and patriotism.
2. Evaluate how you spend your time. Identify three areas where you invest your time and resources, not because you like to or are passionate about it but because you feel you must. Write down what they are and what values are at play when they are performed to the best of your abilities.
3. Reflect on past performance. Look back on events, situations, or high-stakes moments where you performed well and were very satisfied with the outcome. What drove you to perform in these moments?

CHAPTER 2

PRINCIPLES

There is knowing, there is saying, and then there is doing. Knowing what you value is important, but knowing is not enough. We must connect our values with behavior, with action. Hopefully in the previous action steps you were able to flesh out some values that are important to you. Maybe you also identified some values that you need to reach your goals.

Identifying important values is the first step in understanding what drives us to perform on the X. But to execute, we must align those values with actions. If I value friendship, then I demonstrate that value with the principle of always showing up for my friends. I make time for them even when I am tired. I am curious about their lives and prioritize their needs, I follow through with my commitments, and when I can't or fall short, I apologize and make it up to them.

NAVY SEAL PRINCIPLES

The US Navy has principles that align with the values of honor, courage, and commitment. Navy SEALs practice Warrior Toughness values every day, in every way:

Preparation. We are meticulous and consistent in our operational planning and mission rehearsal processes. We are creative and innovative in the development of new tactics and procedures.

Work ethic. The more we sweat in training, the less we bleed in combat. Our effort in training and preparation is what sets us apart. We will set high standards and cut no corners in preparing for war.

Perseverance. We can always improve our fighting position or situation—we are never out of the fight. When we feel the urge to give up or take our foot off the gas, we will tell ourselves that we know we can go further and that our teammates are counting on us.

Teamwork. We can't do great things on our own—it is about the team. We will never leave a man behind. We will pull our weight and expect the same from our teammates.

Very early on in BUD/S training, the organizational values are instilled and demonstrated in principles that we live in training. These principles serve as the very foundation of our development as future SEALs and are some of the most valuable things we learn in BUD/S.

By the time we are near the end of Third Phase (Land Warfare Phase), we are well versed in these very basic principles as they relate to SEAL values.

WARRIOR TOUGHNESS PRINCIPLES AT WORK

The greatest military leadership stories throughout history typically involve the leader setting the heroic example and inspiring his men to execute courageously in the face of extreme difficulty or overwhelming enemy odds. These are not my stories. After a long career in military special operations, many are surprised to find that my greatest leadership challenges were not even on the battlefield. I never had to inspire my guys to act heroically or take the fight to the enemy. SEALs don't need to be led like that. They live for that fight. Performing on the X in this case is often more about digging into your values—in this case, the Navy value of commitment.

Toward the final months of my last Iraq deployment, the operational tempo had started to slow down and the guys started to become restless. The transition from leading SEALs to kick down doors and chase bad guys to asking them to perform in less glamorous roles is a difficult one. They had been hearing the stories about how busy the other SEAL troop was in another part of the country. That SEAL troop had a higher-profile mission with more support assets and intelligence capability thrown at it. It would be dishonest to say that we were not jealous.

Instead of kicking in doors and engaging the enemy, our primary focus shifted to training and professionalizing our Iraqi Special Operations Forces (SOF) partners. As the platoon chief, the senior enlisted leader, I too became dissatisfied with our slower tempo, but I also became frustrated that guys seemed to resist their changing role. They felt that we could be busier if more intelligence assets were diverted our way.

One evening I briefed the platoon on what some of the new roles and responsibilities were, and there was clear grumbling and dissatisfaction in the room. As we started to file out, one of the team leaders spoke up. "Hey, assholes! I would rather be right here doing this job with you guys than over there doing that awesome job with that other troop." To my team leader, it was more about the people around him than the specific task he was engaged in.

That was a pivotal turning point for the end of our deployment. There was still some complaining and jealousy of their friends in the other troop, but the guys leaned into one another and stepped up their professionalism, giving their best in developing the Iraqis' combat capabilities.

It wasn't a dream deployment, but I am proud of how the guys stepped up and finished strong; they performed on the X through their work ethic and teamwork.

PRINCIPLES: PUTTING VALUES INTO ACTION IN A PROFESSIONAL SETTING

I value loyalty and reputation, as I described in my BUD/S story. I feel an obligation to be trustworthy and reliable. Throughout my military career and as a business owner, I've tried to live those values through principled actions.

During my military service, when leaders put their faith and trust in me, I made sure that I understood their intent and expectations. I made decisions and took risks in training and on the battlefield with those things in mind. When I fell short or made mistakes, which happened more often than I care to mention, I was honest and accountable to those I led as well as to my bosses.

Today, when a meeting or event planner hires me for a speaking engagement, they are taking a chance on me. Their name and professional reputation are on the line. People are counting on them to run a smooth event. When I speak professionally, my job is to not only serve the attendees and organization but also make the meeting planner look good. In support of those objectives, a few of the values most important to me are professionalism, dependability, and respect/courteousness.

When I practice those values for a speaking engagement, they look like this:

- My speech is painstakingly rehearsed and delivered with passion and precision. My content reflects the agreed-upon message.
- I am early to all engagements and rehearsals. I do not go over the allotted time for my presentation, even if it means that I must cut my speech short.
- I treat everyone with dignity and respect, whether they're the waiter, support technician, or CEO.

Action Steps: Defining Your Principles

1. Identify and articulate your principles. Now that you have defined your values, how can you put those values into action? What specific actions can you take to support those values?

2. Hold yourself accountable and consider tapping a trusted adviser to also hold you accountable by calling you out when you make decisions or act in a manner that is not in alignment with your values or principles. Solicit feedback from other professional and personal connections. Do people see you acting in alignment with your values? If not, how can you shift your behavior to support the core ideas of who you are and what you are about?

CHAPTER 3

ATTRIBUTES

We all have unique attributes that help us perform under pressure, but when it comes to Warrior Toughness and performing on the X, there are certain qualities or strengths that we need to thrive in our most challenging situations. Obviously, military examples are more extreme than daily life, but the attributes of the Warrior Toughness Program can be applied to your high-stakes moments. They are defined as the ability to

- take a hit and keep going;
- perform under pressure; and
- deal with the "day in, day out" grind.

SIX HOURS IN HELL—THE PREQUEL: ATTRIBUTES OF A REAL-LIFE RAMBO

Do you remember reading about Roy Benavidez in chapter 1? He was a courageous soldier and a committed teammate.

Raul Perez "Roy" Benavidez was born in 1935 in a small town outside Cuero, Texas, to a Mexican farmer and a Yaqui mother. By the time he was seven, both his parents had died of tuberculosis, and he and his brother went to live with extended family in El Campo. As a mixed-race child, he was bullied constantly, and at age fifteen he dropped out of school to help support the family.

In 1952, he joined the Texas Army National Guard and three years later the US Army. Several years after that he would complete the grueling Special Forces Assessment and Selection process and be awarded the coveted Green Beret. In 1965, while on a classified reconnaissance mission in Vietnam, he stepped on a land mine and was seriously wounded, suffering from traumatic brain and spinal injuries. Finally, he was medevaced back to the Army medical hospital in San Antonio and began a long and painful recovery.

The doctors told Sergeant Benavidez that he would never walk again and would be eventually medically discharged. Fueled partly by flag-burning antiwar protestors and seeing his fellow wounded soldiers, Benavidez was determined to prove them wrong and return to combat in Vietnam. Against the medical advice, he began to secretly conduct his own nighttime rehabilitation sessions. In the beginning, he would wiggle his toes, roll out of bed, and drag himself along the floor. Then he gained the strength to slide up the wall and stand. These rehab sessions were absolutely excruciating but eventually paid off. He begged the doctors not to discharge him. One doctor dismissively said that if Benavidez could get up and walk out the door, he would tear up his discharge papers. He did just that, and by 1968 Benavidez was back with Special Forces in Vietnam.

Master Sergeant Benavidez was clearly driven by strong values and principles, but it was key attributes that allowed for such extraordinary action throughout his life. It was resilience, determination, and perseverance that drove him to endure painful rehab in recovery and later to perform heroically under fire while seriously wounded.

THE US NAVY'S TOP ATTRIBUTES

In 2015, Chief of Naval Operations Admiral John M. Richardson released his leadership philosophy, *A Design for Maintaining Maritime Superiority*. Admiral Richardson believed that the most effective military forces were ones that could execute at a high level with a decentralized command structure. Navy leaders and sailors must understand what risk can be tolerated and must be trusted and empowered to execute independently, free of the typical top-down leadership and management processes.

Within the 2018 2.0 *Design*, Admiral Richardson outlined four core attributes that all Navy personnel needed to possess:

- **Integrity:** Our conduct must always be upright and honorable. Our behaviors as individuals, as teams, and as an organization must align with our values as a profession. We will actively strengthen our resolve to act consistently with our values.

- **Accountability:** We are a mission-focused force. We achieve and maintain high standards. Our actions support our strategy. We clearly define the problem we are trying to solve and the outcomes to which we will hold ourselves accountable. In execution, we honestly assess our progress and adjust as required. We are our own toughest critic. Our leaders in command recognize the unique trust and confidence placed in them to operate independently. This is a profound responsibility.

- **Initiative:** We strive to accomplish what needs to be done, even in the absence of direct orders. Leaders at all levels take ownership and act to the limit of their authorities. We foster a questioning attitude, and we encourage everyone to look at new ideas with an open mind. Our most junior teammate may have the best idea; we must be open to capturing and implementing that idea.

- **Toughness:** We can take a hit and keep going, tapping all sources of strength and resilience. Through rigorous training for operations and combat, the fighting spirit of our people, and the steadfast support of our families, we maintain a culture of warfighting excellence and hone our warfighting ethos. We don't give up the ship, we never give up on our shipmates, and we never give up on ourselves. We are never out of the fight.

You also need core attributes that can be applied to your personal and professional life, and these will help you perform on the X. Here are a few basic attributes and qualities to consider:

- **Resilience.** The ability to take a punch or suffer a setback and get back into the fight. We need to respond with right actions and behaviors in the face of loss, challenge, and setbacks.
- **Courage.** Our willingness to commit to action at the risk of receiving criticism, embarrassment, or, in certain cases, personal injury.
- **Perseverance.** The resolve to fight through discomfort, setbacks, and failure to achieve our goals.
- **Poise.** Our ability to maintain composure and focus when under pressure.
- **Integrity.** Live with honor and commit to doing what you say you will.
- **Discipline.** The personal choice to dedicate ourselves to the craft, habits, and skills that enable the successful execution of our goals.
- **Awareness (self and situational).** Self: Our understanding of how our words and actions affect others. Situational: Our ability to grasp situational understanding in context. The ability to see the micro and macro picture while tracking situational changes.
- **Initiative.** Our ability to make sound decisions and take action when needed in the absence of leadership or hands-on guidance.
- **Adaptability.** Our ability to be flexible and adjust to new situations or circumstances.
- **Self-efficacy.** Our belief that we can perform and execute in mission-critical situations.

It would be easy to dismiss the incredible actions of people like Master Sergeant Benavidez as otherworldly or unrelatable, but the fact is Benavidez possessed strength in critical attributes. He had training and committed to bold choices. Most will thankfully never be in extreme situations like the master sergeant, but you can look at these stories as inspiration. You *are* capable of developing the attributes and skills required to perform in your critical and challenging moments.

ATTRIBUTES AT WORK

Let's look at a nonmilitary example of Warrior Toughness attributes in action.

Sheryl was a high-performing sales representative. She sold ortho-pedic replacement devices, and as the subject matter expert, she was required to scrub in for surgery and advise the doctor and surgical team. She knew her stuff inside and out, was respected by the doctors, and had great sales numbers.

When a district sales manager position opened up, Sheryl seemed like the natural choice, so she applied and was selected for the po-sition. Within six months, another device competitor had emerged and began cutting into her company's market share. To make mat-ters worse, Sheryl's team lagged behind many of her company's other teams' sales numbers.

As the pressure on Sheryl and her team mounted, she became increasingly hands-on with the sales reps on her team. Rather than providing leadership through coaching and resourcing, Sheryl took on the role of a "super-rep," demanding that her team conduct busi-ness as she had done during her time as a sales rep. For a myriad of reasons, this approach is seldom an effective strategy for a manager. When tasks and procedures were not handled in the manner and with the speed that she expected, she became increasingly more frustrated. Her emails and phone conversations became terse and were not well received by her team. They began to feel micromanaged and, at the same time, unsupported.

Qualities, or attributes, that enabled Sheryl to succeed as a high-performing sales rep did not immediately show up or were not trans-ferred to her new position as a leader and manager. Her inability to lead in this new role and manage its stressors manifested in the quali-ties of low self-awareness, micromanagement, and lack of adaptability.

We are born with innate personality traits that endow us with certain positive attributes but do not confer others. Leadership at-tributes, like most other qualities, can be developed and improved, provided there is the willingness to do so. Though Sheryl was not suc-cessfully leading her team, she actually possessed strong leadership attributes that would build and improve upon the weaker ones. First and foremost, she was humble and committed to being a better leader.

Sheryl knew she needed help with improving her leadership skills and had the courage and humility to ask for 360-degree feedback. She asked her subordinates, superiors, and peers alike to give her feedback on her leadership and management abilities.

With this valuable feedback and through coaching, Sheryl began to turn the ship around by developing other important leadership at-tributes, such as adaptability, self-awareness, trust, and resilience.

Adaptability. Part of learning how to be a new leader is under-standing that your leadership style and technique must be adapted to each situation and individual. Different situations call for different in-terventions, and individuals need to be led in different ways. Sheryl learned that some members of her team had unique challenges specific to their territory, so they war-gamed strategy to tackle them together.

Self-awareness. Sheryl's subordinates were also feeling the pres-sure of lagging numbers, so Sheryl had to be very conscious of how her email and conversational language would be received. Her tone needed to be one that picked up and inspired the team, not one that conveyed her own personal stress.

Trust. Despite their challenges, Sheryl knew she had a capable team. She came to terms with the fact that each team member had their own methods and strategies for sales. Sheryl learned how to hold people accountable while also empowering and supporting their in-dividual styles. She also learned that part of building trust with those you lead is being known as a manager who leads up and pushes back on leadership when they make decisions that negatively affect the teams in the field.

Resilience. Rather than reacting to the pressure she was facing, as she had been, Sheryl now worked on skills and strategies that would enable her to respond to challenges and bounce back from setbacks. Sheryl now viewed challenge as an opportunity to demonstrate resil-ience and resolve.

ATTRIBUTES IN WORK AND LIFE

Your values and principles can galvanize your resolve and drive your commitment to thrive and perform on the X. Identifying which attributes are important in a given situation and which ones need further development will enable you to live out these values.

As an example, I found that during my time as a SEAL operator, I could stay focused and engaged in stressful situations regarding combat and combat-related training—I was adaptable and resilient. Yet, in my daily life, I would often struggle to bring that same clarity and self-regulation to events involving family stressors or that jerk who just cut me off in traffic. I was not as adaptive as I needed to be. I needed to look at stress and challenge in a more general sense. I needed to consistently apply certain psychology skills to *all* aspects of life that presented challenges. Only when I did this could I raise my A game across the board.

Action Steps: Developing Your Attributes for Life on the X

When it comes to bringing your A game to important and critical moments, Warrior Toughness attributes are a good starting point. You may be fairly strong in these or need further development.

1. Reflective exercise. Take twenty minutes and go for a walk, or sit in a quiet room and reflect on more recent high-stakes or stressful situations. Think about how you performed. In a nonjudgmental way, be candid in your assessment.

2. Evaluation. Based on this reflective exercise and other past experiences, rate your level of strength on a scale of 1 to 10 in the following attributes:

- Resilience
- Courage
- Perseverance
- Poise
- Integrity
- Discipline
- Awareness (self and situational)
- Initiative
- Adaptability
- Self-efficacy

Which attributes do you want to further strengthen? How can you practice improving these attributes?

3. **Feedback.** Develop a 360-degree feedback assessment to help gauge your strengths and weaknesses.[1] Ask those you trust to give you honest and helpful feedback geared toward your growth and development.

---

1. For a great read and a deeper dive into the subject of attributes, I highly recommend Rich Diviney's book *The Attributes: 25 Hidden Drivers of Optimal Performance*. See Rich's appendix for a list of drivers.

CHAPTER 4

PURPOSE

As a young kid who loved playing "army" in the woods, I carried a lot of that with me when I made the decision to join the US Navy to be a SEAL. When I finally got orders to BUD/S and arrived, I quickly questioned my purpose in being there. Prior to that I was focused on the challenge as well as thoughts of crawling around with my face painted green and generally doing cool-guy commando stuff. When the training started to get really hard, those reasons didn't seem like enough to keep me there. While accomplishing the challenges of some of the hardest military training in the world was still valid, I needed something greater.

What I connected to was the fact that I was surrounded by some of the best men that I had ever met, and I felt like I had a home. As our training class progressed over time, we developed those strong bonds forged by adversity. In the Teams we refer to it as a *brotherhood*. That brotherhood became my ultimate sense of purpose and essentially got me through training and my subsequent military career. Purpose is the drive behind your values and principles.

PURPOSE (MISSING) IN ACTION

John was one of my good friends at BUD/S. He was a former Navy diver and performed well at pretty much everything we did. By the time we got to Hell Week, a week in SEAL training most notorious for suffering and DORs (*drop on requests*—the Navy term for quitting in training), we had known each other for almost eight weeks and so I felt I knew him pretty well. I must admit that there were plenty of times that I lacked confidence in training and he was a great guy to lean on. By Wednesday morning of Hell Week it is very rare for anyone to quit. You are so sleep-deprived that you are on autopilot. You also take on a defiant "screw you" attitude to the instructors because you are so invested, there is nothing more that they can do to you to make you quit.

That morning we had woken up from our naps in dry clothing. I say "nap" because we were only given a few hours of sleep for the entire week. We had also not remained in dry clothing for that long up to this point. We were quickly told to hit the surf. This meant running into the cold Pacific surf, followed by rolling around in the sand to make it even more miserable.

As we ran to form up in our boat crews for the next torturous event, I looked for John but did not see him. I turned and asked another classmate if he had seen him. "Yup, he quit," he said casually. "What?" I said with astonishment. He described, with a chuckle, how after waking up and being told to hit the surf, John looked down at his warm and dry clothing and simply said, "Nope." He DOR'd on the spot. Unlike my classmate, I was not amused. I was surprised and also disappointed. I didn't have long to dwell on it, though, and moved on.

The following Monday, after our class finished Hell Week, I ran into John while he was on a cleanup detail. When I asked him what had happened, he said he just couldn't believe that he had quit. I ran into him a few more times over the next couple of years, and each time he seemed pained by his decision. I don't know if John would have made a great SEAL; others have quit and made it through training a second time, though. I do know that he was smart enough and fit enough to get through the rest of training if he hadn't quit that day. John lost his way because, while he knew what he wanted, he was not connected strongly enough to his purpose.

WHEN PURPOSE IS TESTED: DO I EVEN MATTER HERE?

Early in my career as a SEAL, deployed SEAL platoons would spend a lot of time aboard ships; before 9/11 we would often be attached to amphibious assault ships or aircraft carriers in support of that task or carrier group. These were considered undesirable deployments, and fortunately for me, I only had to do one deployment attached to a ship, and even then we didn't spend much time aboard. After 9/11, we spent less time on ships and most of that time was for brief training scenarios or short combat operations. During my career as a SEAL, I spent much more time around the Army than I did with the Navy, outside of Naval Special Warfare, of course. Finishing up my career at the Navy's boot camp was really an eye-opening experience for me. It was here that I started to understand what the challenges of a real Navy sailor are.

One day after teaching a Warrior Toughness lesson, I struck up a conversation with a hull maintenance technician (HT) chief petty officer. An HT is essentially a Navy plumber and welder. The Navy chief petty officer, or chief, is a senior noncommissioned officer and is referred to as the backbone of the Navy.

This chief began to tell me about one difficult deployment he had as a young sailor on board an amphibious assault ship. This is essentially an aircraft carrier for helicopters that includes a large force of embarked marines and their amphibious landing vehicles. The young petty officer was assigned to an engineering space where he performed repairs and maintenance deep within the bowels of the ship. On this particular deployment, his ship was assigned to the Mediterranean Sea area of operations. He was well into a six-month deployment and the ship seemed to do little else but turn in large squares in the middle of the ocean. There were a few port calls and the embarked marines would conduct routine exercises, but for this young sailor it was monotonous: every day was Groundhog Day.

Unfortunately, while he was at sea, his young wife was home getting ready to give birth to their first child. He was missing the birth of his firstborn . . . for what? He thought, "What's so important about what I'm doing that it warrants missing the birth of my first baby?" His bosses seemed somewhat sympathetic and just told him the Navy really needed him there. He became increasingly more disillusioned with his job. He missed his wife and was sick about missing the birth, but most of all he lacked purpose.

We cannot be fully committed without a strong sense of purpose.

Our young sailor's leadership team failed to fill that void for him during this time. The chief described how he felt that his leaders showed basic compassion for him missing the birth, but they missed an opportunity to reframe his situation and motivate him to see the vital role that all sailors and marines on that vessel played in securing vital strategic interests for the United States. They failed to challenge and inspire or support him with additional mentoring, leadership development, or other professional development opportunities. Had he been given that, he would have still felt the sting of the sacrifice he was making, but he would have been much more invested in his job and in the people he worked with. We in the military accept that we must make great sacrifices, but we need for them to mean something.

Our young sailor resolved to get out of the Navy as soon as his enlistment was up. Fortunately, he was given an opportunity for another assignment, one that saw him with new leadership. This new leadership inspired and challenged him, helping him find that sense of purpose that he desperately needed to see the value in his actions and contributions to the team and mission.

Today, that chief petty officer is determined to help all sailors under his leadership find that sense of purpose and keep it when they get tested. He does that by connecting what they do to the bigger picture. He invests his time getting to know them and giving them what they need professionally, sometimes whether they want it or not. By getting to know his sailors, he knows what motivates them, how hard he can push them, and when they need some compassion and support when things get hard. When a deployment gets monotonous, he provides extra training and gives increased levels of responsibility to junior sailors.

FINDING PURPOSE IN YOUR WORK

In a perfect world we love the organization and customers we serve. We believe strongly in the mission and it drives us. We are part of a well-gelled team, and we love to show up to work every day. I hope some of these things are true for you, but the reality is that even when we love what we do, there are days and times when we feel disconnected, when we doubt ourselves. Even when we really like our organization, there will be times that we question the decisions made or the direction the company is going. We may not like our boss.

I would venture to say that there have been times in your life when you have struggled to find purpose or drive and felt unmotivated in your life and hated doing what you were doing. In cases like these, having a strong sense of purpose can make all the difference.

As individuals, we must take ownership in connecting to purpose. We must validate and often revalidate this sense of purpose. As leaders and teammates, we can and should be instrumental in helping do this for others. Our organization and customers deserve it, but most of all we deserve it. We deserve to have purpose in our lives and in our work.

For us to be committed, tough, resilient, and ultimately successful in the face of challenge and hardship, we must be resolute in our purpose. We must have something that drives us in adding value and bringing our best selves to our profession and our relationships. We, ourselves, are all ultimately responsible for finding that purpose in our work and pursuits. That said, we cannot minimize the role that we as teammates and leaders play. In those roles we must remember that we often serve as the vital instruments for helping to validate or revalidate that sense of purpose in others.

LIVING WITH PURPOSE: CALCULATIONS AND COMPROMISE

It was early January 2014. I had just finished a tour where I served and deployed as a SEAL troop senior-enlisted adviser, or troop chief, as we call it. I was the senior enlisted to lead for two eighteen-man SEAL platoons. It was a significant leadership milestone, and for the most part I really enjoyed it. I felt that I did a pretty good job but still had a fair share of things that I wish I'd done better. I thought about some of the mistakes I made and how much better I could do if I had a chance to do the job again. In almost every instance, a successful completion of this milestone meant I would never get that chance.

It was my eight-year-old son's first year of travel ice hockey. Our team was in the very southeast corner of Virginia, and most of the other teams in our league were several hours away in Maryland and northern Virginia. Almost every other weekend meant a road trip up north for Saturday and Sunday games. The coach and I were good friends, and we rode up to these games together. Having never played the sport myself, I was surprised by how much joy these travel weekends brought me. Between watching my kid play and hanging out with the other hockey dads, I was having a blast.

At the time, I was at headquarters in a staff job. One day, the headquarters operations master chief approached me and asked if I would like to do another troop chief spot at the command I had just left; one of the other troop chiefs was being fired and they needed someone to fill the spot. I loved being a SEAL, specifically the training and deployment overseas. This was my chance to get my wish to repeat and crush it the second time around. I told him I would mull it over with the family and get back to him.

Sacrifice and compromise are seldom talked about in this context when discussing the pursuit of passion and finding purpose in the work we do. When we are young with few attachments and responsibilities, we can pursue our passions with reckless abandon. As we get older and our priorities change, the responsibilities grow and we must place our professional pursuits against the backdrop of a greater purpose.

In the end, I turned down that second troop chief spot and stayed in my somewhat-boring staff job. During my career, up to that point, I was passionately connected to my purpose as a SEAL operator. My family always came second. But I had grown and developed, and my purpose had shifted. I ended up making almost every one of my son's games and have zero regrets about the choice I made. As far as the staff job, I did my very best and am proud and satisfied with some of the things that I was able to accomplish.

Our purpose has to be greater than the job or task that we do. You must be more than what you do. Our professional pursuits are our opportunity to demonstrate our values and principles as well as our passions. Can you be counted on to perform on the X when things get hard, or can I count on you only when you're properly motivated and you feel like it?

IT'S ON YOU

In a perfect world we are completely aligned with our company's mission at all times. We are all in and connected with the "just cause" of our organization, as author Simon Sinek would say; we believe in how we fit and contribute.

Even if that might be true for us, again, it does not mean things will always be rosy. We might not always like the direction that our organization takes. We may not care for the leadership; we may deal with difficult teammates. This is likely to happen even in our dream jobs.

Being resolute in our sense of purpose does not mean that seemingly hard things will now become easier or that we will suddenly be motivated when things are not going well. Having a strong sense of purpose is one of the foundational ingredients that keep us on course and enable us to make the right decisions and behave in the right way, regardless of circumstances.

When all else fails, when we don't have leaders that inspire us, when we don't have a team that we can lean on for support, it remains up to us to find that drive and purpose. For me, Steve Drum the businessperson, this is who I am and this is what I stand for:

- I am a professional.
- I do for others.
- I am committed to excellence.
- I will make mistakes, but I am not a person who quits; I will only get better.
- I choose to see opportunity in *all* situations—no matter how difficult.

It is the role of a leader to inspire and motivate when necessary. A good leader needs to do this, but this book is about you owning your ability to be your best self and not relying on others to give you purpose in what you do. It's on you.

Action Steps: Finding Your Purpose

1. Define your greatest purpose. Think, in the most general sense, of what drives you and how you contribute to people and situations.
2. Define your professional purpose. Identify what drives and excites you in your work. Be clear on how what you do adds value to the organizational mission, the customer, and those around you.
3. Define your relational purpose. Just like with greater and professional purpose, relational purpose is about adding value. It's about adding value to the people in our lives: our families, friends, and coworkers.

CHAPTER 5

CHARACTER

Character is our adherence to morals, principles, and beliefs. We cannot expect to successfully navigate life's challenges and obstacles and get where we need to be without a solid moral compass. Through intense reflection, and even consultation with those we respect, we must discover the values, principles, and beliefs that we really connect with and buy into.

In the military, preparing young men and women for combat and the rigors of Navy life requires much more than just skills and professional knowledge. When warfighters face extreme challenge and adversity in combat, or what life in general throws at them, they need to be able to stand on the solid foundation of values, principles, morals, and beliefs. It is this foundation that is the essence of their character. That strength of character is critical to perform on the X, in the military and in daily life.

In the SEAL Teams, we look for people who can buy into something greater than themselves. We need loyalty that is balanced with moral courage. We are fully committed to our brothers and sisters in arms and are willing to pay the ultimate sacrifice for them if need be. We are loyal to our teammates, but our ultimate loyalty must be toward our code and organizational ethics. In practice, this is one of the most difficult aspects of being a SEAL leader; there are lines that cannot be crossed. A soldier or sailor with strong character knows how to align their personal morals and values with the organization and mission.

CHARACTER REVEALED

There is a popular expression in the SEAL Teams that you first hear in BUD/S: "Everyone wants to be a frogman [SEAL] on a sunny day." Part of the reason that SEAL training and selection is so difficult is because of the harsh environments and conditions we are expected to work under. It's one thing to perform and execute in calm seas, it's quite another to lead and execute in adverse, complex, and highly challenging conditions. That goes for pain and discomfort, but also making difficult or unpopular decisions in the face of criticism. It is here that our strength of character is tested and ultimately revealed. If we are truly committed to being our best selves in the situations and for the people that matter most in our lives, we must be people of solid character.

There are skills and practices that can prepare us for adverse situations and help with our resilience, but it is the strength of character that allows us to stay engaged with our short- and long-term goals. The character work you are doing here is the foundation that prepares you to perform through adversity and challenge.

CONSISTENCY OF CHARACTER

While you may be cool as a cucumber and excel in one area or set of situations, you may not carry that same poise and focus into the other areas of your life.

The years I spent as a SEAL operator had taken their toll. I was reluctant to seek help because I compared myself to those who I felt had "real" injuries. The amputees, the multiple gunshot wounds, those that had been through very serious emotional trauma. I felt that I had no room to complain. The reality, though, was that I had been exposed to events that impacted me. I had been exposed to explosive blasts in combat as well as thousands of blasts in training as an operator and instructor.

I was not sleeping very well and was frequently angry or quick to anger, and I constantly felt on edge or on guard. I did not like the person I had become, and it was severely affecting my marriage; it was also spilling over to my professional life.

One afternoon, I was in my front yard with my wife, mother-in-law, and two children. They were playing and talking while I did some trivial yard work. At some point the kids started to bicker, and I lost my temper. I yelled at them in a way that was not proportional to their behavior. My wife stepped in to scold me and I snapped at her too.

After I cooled down, my mother-in-law approached me. The two of us are very close, and when she gives me advice and guidance, I almost always take it on board. She went on to tell me how my children were observing and learning from my behavior. What was I teaching them, and how would they think of me as a father?

I was setting a poor example and not effectively leading in my home. I was neither the father nor the husband that I needed to be. I had to make some changes. Being a person of character often requires the wisdom to see where your gaps are and having the willingness to fill them by getting the help you need in the areas where you need it.

CHARACTER: ALIGNING VALUES WITH BEHAVIOR

When I became aware of the way my behavior was out of line with my morals and values (character!), I decided to take action.

There is a grant-funded program in Bethesda, Maryland, that treats service members with post-traumatic stress and traumatic brain injury. I was admitted into the program and underwent four weeks of treatment there. PTS and TBI were your ticket for admission to the program, but once in there you were evaluated from head to toe. A panel of doctors and staff members conferred on how they could best treat your entire person, holistically, versus the more typical specialized care.

I was treated with the standard interventions of mental health, occupational health, testing with psychologists, and brain scans. What was so fascinating and unusual was that the program would hit you with any and all types of alternative treatments in the hope that it would help. We did art and music therapy. We did acupuncture and yoga. It was here that I was exposed to mental training for the first time, including meditation and performance psychology techniques.

This was amazing but still no magic bullet. I had much work to do to get myself operating in a better space. That work continues to this day. The humility, courage, and will to make real change takes character.

We need to identify the important areas and moments in our lives and where we can improve. More importantly, we need to identify the areas where there are gaps or shortcomings and give them serious attention.

The most important areas in our lives are often where our character is tested and revealed the most. It is in these moments where we must be deeply connected and driven by our values, principles, and beliefs.

Action Steps: The Strength of Your Character

The point of part 1 of this book is for you to fully invest and commit to whatever it takes to be your best self and perform on the X. As you have moved through the previous chapters, we have assembled the requisite pieces to do this. The values that you hold, the principles that you live, and the purpose that drives you are all parts of your character. The strength of your character determines your ability to adhere to those things in the face of challenge and adversity.

1. List the situations in your personal life that test your character. Do you live your principles in social situations? Do

you respond to challenges in your relationships with the actions and behavior that you are happy with?

2. List the professional situations in your life that test your character. Do your personal morals and beliefs align with organizational values and ethics? Do you respond to stressful or challenging situations in a way that you are proud of?

3. Write down one or two sentences on how you would like a family member to describe your sense of character. How do you want to be seen by them?

CHAPTER 6

COMMITMENT

For many of us, there are high-stakes moments that we live for, that we seem to thrive in. Whatever stress we feel sharpens our focus and elevates our performance. When you are engaged in this activity, you don't necessarily feel distressed or overwhelmed.

Even if you feel that you thrive in these moments, you are reading this book because you are serious about elevating your performance, and if you are being honest with yourself, you probably realize that there is room for improvement. If you are like me, you feel strong in certain areas while realizing there are gaps in other areas that must be addressed.

WARRIOR TOUGHNESS TAKES COMMITMENT

One of the final jobs I had in the US Navy before I retired was to oversee the Dive Motivator Division at the Recruit Training Command (Navy Boot Camp, as it is commonly called). Our job was to help onboard new basic training recruits that had a Special Operations or Special Warfare contract; the contract ensured that if they passed the physical fitness screening test and the medical exam, they would get a chance to move on to the next stage of their program's training pipeline upon successful graduation.

Training programs included contracts for SEAL, Special Warfare combatant-craft crewmen, explosive ordnance disposal (EOD) technicians, divers, and aviation rescue swimmers. These programs were prestigious, and all of them had rigorous selection and training processes; SEAL training had the highest attrition rates.

Anywhere from 75 to 90 percent of SEAL candidates who start the program wash out before graduation.

Our job was to put them through progressive run, swim, and calisthenic training to get them stronger, faster on their feet, and more comfortable in the water. Between boot camp and the assessment and selection process, Basic Underwater Demolition/SEAL Training or BUD/S, these candidates received far more physical preparation training than our generation of SEALs ever had. These candidates were stronger, faster, and better in the water than we ever were. Yet, despite all this extra preparation, the attrition rate remained the same. For years, psychologists and other experts have been trying to crack the formula of why some candidates succeed when others do not.

Getting inside the candidate's head, we felt, could help make a difference in some of these candidates being successful. The best way for us to do this was with frequent mentoring sessions. When I would conduct mentoring sessions with a new boot camp division of SEAL candidates, I would always start out with a little shock and awe.

This was a version of my introductory speech:

> Most of you will not make it. Most of you will never graduate and become SEALs (pause for dramatic effect).
>
> Why do you think most of you will be unsuccessful? (No matter which class or division or recruits that I asked, I typically got the same responses:)
>
> "Not in good enough shape."
>
> "Not good enough in the water."
>
> Yes, some of you may not be fit enough, not good enough in the water. Some will get injured. Some will

fail evolutions and be dropped from training. Yes, this will happen to some of you, no doubt.

The reality is, most of you will be unsuccessful, not for those reasons but because when things start to get hard, when pain sets in, when faced with doubt, you will discover that the price of admission into our community is more than what you are willing to pay.

You are excited right now with the prospect of being a SEAL. You may envision yourself jumping out of a plane, kicking doors in, or blowing things up . . . all the fun stuff. The problem, though, is that when it's time to put in the work, you will discover that you are not as committed as you thought you were and you will ring the bell. You will look to find an easier path in life. Being a SEAL is definitely not for everyone.

I was surrounded by incredible athletes when I was at BUD/S, but I succeeded where many of them failed because I could do what those who failed could not.

I knew how to commit. I knew how to take my values, principles, and purpose and successfully align them with my goals.

COMMITMENT AT HOME AND AT WORK

I felt more at ease dealing with stress and crisis in a combat and high-risk training environment than I did in my personal life. Professionally, there was plenty of room to improve my game as well. I can parade out the excuses of the stress of multiple combat deployments, getting poor sleep, and other medical issues I had going on, but that's all it would be—excuses.

I needed to raise my game and perform better as a father and a husband. The tools were there from my SEAL training and leadership, but I did not yet know how to use them consistently across all the areas of my life. When I helped create the Warrior Toughness Program, it was essential that the skills we taught could be framed and translated to all areas of one's professional and personal life.

HOW TO COMMIT WHEN YOUR CHARACTER IS TESTED

There are times when life seems like one series of hardships after another; you must come to terms with hardship. As the ancient Greek and Roman Stoics preached, there is opportunity in all things, even in loss, failure, and pain. Sometimes that opportunity is as simple as demonstrating grace, resolve, or compassion. There is great virtue in that. When you are challenged, focus only on what you can control. Take satisfaction in being your best self in that situation—independent of the actual outcome. When I practice embracing opportunity, I work to strengthen my character and renew my commitment every day and will continue to do that until I die. So should you.

When we face a challenge to our character, we must do three things:

1. We must hold ourselves accountable. We must have the commitment and integrity to own and admit our mistakes.
2. We must forgive ourselves. We are human and will miss the mark more often than we would like. There are times when we may not receive forgiveness or acceptance by others, but for us there is no other choice but to move forward.
3. We must reframe our mistakes into the behavior and choices that get us moving in the right direction. Focus on what we must do and not on what we *should* or should *not* have done.

A SEAL Team Leader's Mission Statement

Having a strong mission statement that connects our values with principled behavior and decisions does not make us immune from stumbling and setbacks. I, like you, will fall short of making principled decisions at times. There will be situations where my behavior may not be in alignment with my personal philosophy. It is critical that we reconcile this; otherwise, we risk throwing up our hands and giving up, thinking ourselves frauds. Here is my mission statement:

- I am a humble professional (I treat everyone I encounter with dignity and respect and follow through with my commitments).
- I work to get better every day (even if just a little bit).
- In my professional life, I work to improve my writing, branding, and speech performance.
- In my personal life, I work to be a better husband and father. I am committed to mental and physical fitness.
- I don't crumble when things get hard; I focus on what I can control. Life is a series of hardships and challenges. I will look for opportunity in *all* situations and not waste my time wringing my hands over things I cannot affect.
- I exist to be of service and do for those around me. My life has been about service and will continue to be so. I must be committed to help others as I have been helped. People in my life depend on me, and I won't let them down.

Action Steps: Write a Mission Statement That You Are Committed To

As part of the Warrior Toughness Program, I would ask SEAL candidates to create a personal philosophy, or mission statement. This mission statement would flesh out their values and beliefs and give them solid footing that they could turn to when they faced doubt. This simple exercise was an important part of Warrior Toughness, and it's something that I continue to employ today in my coaching and workshops. It is designed to help you clearly define *what* you are committing to in order to perform on the X in your professional and personal life. Reviewing the action steps below and crafting a personal mission statement will be the culmination of all the work you have done in part 1 of this book.

1. Return to the action steps in the previous chapters and compile your key

    *   values,
    *   principles, and
    *   attributes (your strengths and aspirational strengths, or areas for improvements).

    Pro tip: When doing work like this, I often find it helpful to write on a vertical surface by using a whiteboard or color-coded sticky notes.

2. Create your personal mission statement(s). It is OK to have a more focused professional version as well as a more general one for the other parts of your life.

This may take several iterations until you have something that you are happy with. This philosophy should be placed where you can see it, and you should have it committed to memory. I highly encourage you to share this with your trusted advisers and mentors. Check in and request of them that they hold you accountable to your mission statement and what it contains.

Part 2

COMMIT

REFLECT   X   **PREPARE**

EXECUTE

There are several primary factors that enable the success of SEALs and other special operations units. Special Operations Forces (SOF) enjoy rigorous and thorough assessment and selection processes, ensuring the nation's finest and most capable men and women serve in these specialized units. SOF units have a budget that allows for realistic and frequent training with cutting-edge military equipment. SOF operators are meticulous in their planning and creative and innovative in development of tactics.

Despite these important contributing elements, there is one critical factor that enables success when the stakes are the highest. This dirt-simple principle is one that we all can and should embrace. This concept is the need to be exceptionally well prepared—to be brilliant on the basics in terms of tactical preparation. There are some very crafty operators that leave one marveling at their creativity when it comes to solving tactical problems, but it is a reliance on the basics performed extremely well that often carries the day when one is engaged with the enemy or in challenging conditions.

But preparation involves much more than mechanical precision; it's about being mentally prepared to manage energy, emotions, and reactions in any situation.

In 2006, during the surge of troops forwarded to Iraq to turn the tide on sectarian violence, Navy SEALs were badly needed, and the community was looking to grow the force. Naval Special Warfare leadership wanted to know how they could get more SEALs through the training pipeline and onto the battlefield, all while keeping their incredibly high standards. One of the areas that drew attention was an important test evolution for pool competency, or pool comp, as it's called. Pool comp is conducted several weeks into Second Phase (Dive Phase) of BUD/S and is widely considered the second most difficult hurdle after Hell Week to overcome. Pool comp is the culmination of five days of learning basic scuba diving techniques in a nine-foot swimming pool. During the test, trainees are subjected to an intense, high-pressure training environment where breathing hoses are tied in knots and other equipment is tampered with. The trainee must fight panic and distraction while calmly problem-solving. At the time, only one-third of all candidates were making it through the training. These were men who completed Hell Week and were tough as nails, fully committed to their teammates and the program itself; the problem was that many trainees just couldn't perform under that type of pressure. Insisting that no standards be lowered, the instructors and command psychologists employed sports, or performance, psychology techniques that have served elite athletes and helped them handle the pressure of competition for years. They employed some very basic but effective techniques, and before long the failure rate went from only one-third making it to two-thirds successfully passing. The training center had demonstrated that mental skills techniques were highly effective, and today mental skills training is a significant part of how SEALs train for combat. These basic techniques are some of the same ones we use to great success in the Warrior Toughness Program. The techniques outlined are a basic starting point, but they can be employed easily and effectively for your most challenging situations. In this section of the book, I share with you tools and techniques to effectively manage your responses in stressful situations.

CHAPTER 7

OBJECTIVES

The framework in this book will increase your ability to perform under pressure in most areas of your professional and personal life. However, you simply don't have the time, or likely the energy, to develop the knowledge, skills, and attributes to be your best in *every* situation—it's not realistic. Instead, you need to identify and prioritize your efforts toward the most critical periods and situations.

When it comes to performing on the X, objectives drive preparation. This may seem like the most obvious part of what you have read so far, but it bears serious consideration on your part. What are the true objectives of the endeavor you are pursuing?

PREPARING TO ACHIEVE YOUR ULTIMATE OBJECTIVE

Michael Cuddyer enjoyed a very successful fifteen-year career as a Major League Baseball player and two-time all-star, among numerous other awards. Not only making it but having a long and successful career in professional sports takes incredible commitment. Michael would tell you that drive and talent are not nearly enough; he was crystal clear on his objective and worked toward it relentlessly.

From a young age I was obsessed with being and appearing as a professional, or how I thought one would look and act. Even as an amateur, I would say, "I'm a pro." At a young age, everything I did in middle school or high school was to stay true to that core belief that I was a pro.

Our choices and decisions are a direct reflection of who we are and what our core beliefs and principles are. As a high school player, I didn't go to parties because that's not what a pro would do. A pro puts in extra work to go above and beyond and is not satisfied with good enough. A pro will still practice baseball during the football season. During away games in high school, when I stepped off the bus, my uniform was neat, my shirt tucked in. My shoes were clean and my hat was straight because that's what a pro would look like. Later, when I faced adversity in my life, I responded like a pro would. A pro does not get rattled when things don't go their way.

IMMEDIATE (TACTICAL) AND ULTIMATE (STRATEGIC) OBJECTIVES: TOGETHER IS BETTER

In the planning stages of a military ground combat operation, the unit commander will provide his or her commander's intent. This intent describes the desired end state and criteria for success at completion of the operation. It will describe operational limitations and constraints such as rules of engagement and task organization. It is essential that all soldiers on that operation understand what the mission-essential tasks and desired end state of the operation are.

In the field the soldiers/operators are often completely fixated on the tactical objectives of the operation. If Special Operations Forces are going after a specific personnel target, the operators will do everything in their power to accomplish that objective, barring some unforeseen set of circumstances like a helicopter crash or something large and catastrophic in nature. In most cases, the tactical objectives of a particular operation must be placed against the backdrop of a larger theater or country strategy.

In support of the country strategy, toward the end of the Iraq War most of the SOF objective was to develop the capability and capacity of the host nation's SOF units. Additionally, it was essential that the local populace see the indigenous forces as the face of the operation, with US SOF in the background, in a supporting role, seen less as an occupying force and more as supporting partners. Though this was very frustrating for junior operators to come to terms with, the later stages of the war meant that the tactical objectives of many operations were less important than the overall strategic or long-term objectives of our partner forces' capability and credibility with the citizens.

Capturing or killing mid- to lower-level bad guys may not be furthering your long-term objectives if it comes at the cost of excessive collateral damage or minimizing the contributions of the Iraqi or Afghan partner force.

It often takes mindfulness and self-regulation to stay on the path to your objectives. Whether you are giving feedback to a subordinate, correcting your child, or convincing a client, keep both the tactical and strategic objectives in mind. Ensure that the former does not negatively affect the latter without good cause. When working with sales teams, I often discuss how the immediate transaction or agenda (tactical) should not come at the cost of the long-term relationship (strategic).

PROBLEMS AND OBSTACLES: TROUBLESHOOTING TACTICAL AND STRATEGIC OBJECTIVES

As with any military operation, you are well served when you take time to identify a problem or potential obstacle in the way of your objective at the outset. Of those particular obstacles, which are the most challenging? Which ones are likely to cause distress or, more importantly, completely derail your ultimate objective? These critical areas demand our focus. If we can attain readiness and feel confident in meeting the most challenging situations, then the more routine scenarios will be managed with comparative ease.

Most of our training in the SEAL Teams was broken into focus areas. Because SEAL stands for sea, air, and land, we had to train for missions in these three areas. There is a lot of overlap in these areas, but most of our training was broken into two- to five-week blocks. The culmination of these blocks were realistic training scenarios. After we did reps and sets of the basic skills and tactics, we would perform them in complex and drawn-out scenarios. We were almost always given the worst-possible obstacles to overcome. Multiple killed and wounded, downed helicopters, and heavy enemy fire. The human targets we were after would often be spread out in various locations, requiring us to problem-solve on the fly and divide our forces. We would often fall flat on our faces and fail before the instructor staff would give us another opportunity to attempt the mission and succeed. If we can face the biggest challenges in training, everything we face in combat will hopefully be easier.

GOAL-SETTING: TACTICAL OBJECTIVES

Goal-setting is really a way to frame your tactical objectives. My job here is to simplify goal-setting in a way that will help you perform better and get you where you need to be.

Goals should serve to motivate, challenge, hold us accountable, and flesh out strategies for execution. Achieving goals, like many things in life, comes with obstacles sometimes beyond our control. If we are working in sales or marketing, we don't control government regulations, supply chain issues, or other external factors. We want to have goals that motivate and challenge us, but we need to pursue these goals in a manner that serves us.

A professional athlete will typically have large goals such as winning a title, the Super Bowl, or the Stanley Cup—this would be the ultimate objective. Within those, there are also performance goals such as rushing yards or runs batted in—the tactical objectives.

Just like a pro athlete, our ultimate objectives give us direction and purpose but are not the things we should be thinking about on the X. When on the X, we are focused on the tactics and skills that contribute to the desired outcome—we've got to do one in order to achieve the other.

Be SMART about your goal-setting. There are many different goal-setting theories and strategies such as objectives and key results and other stretch-type goals. Many of these are highly effective, or at least useful in the organizational business setting. When it comes to personal growth and performance development, it pays to have a strategy that is a proven performance technology technique, a technique that motivates and inspires through direction and target outcome.

The SMART acronym for goals was developed as a business tool in the early 1980s by consultant George T. Doran. What the letters refer to has been modified into what is commonly used today. There is a good chance that you know this model or have at least heard about it.

Specific. Be crystal clear on what your objectives and outcomes are as well as the conditions and situations that you face.

Measurable. You need to not only measure your overall outcome but be able to build in waypoints or checkpoints for you to measure on the path toward your goal. The sooner and more frequently you can do this, the more efficient your efforts will be.

Attainable. SMART goals should challenge us but be realistic for us to achieve. You will more than likely take your foot off the gas and lose motivation if you realize that your goals are beyond reach.

Relevant. The goals you set should be clearly tied to an overall objective or larger desired outcome. The actions that you execute within the goal pursuit must clearly align with that goal. They should not only align but give the biggest bang for your buck in terms of your time and resource investment.

Time-based. Hold your feet to the fire and make yourself accountable by giving yourself a deadline to meet your goal. Without this time constraint, research says we are less likely to follow through on our goals and actually meet them.

GET CHUNKY

We are usually best served when we take a larger goal or desired outcome and chunk it down into much smaller goals. We may have a revenue goal of $1 million or a quarterly sales goal that we want to hit. We may want to do an Ironman race in a certain time or simply lose X amount of weight by next summer. Take those big-picture goals and chunk them down into bite-size pieces that you can apply hyper-focus to.

SMART Example

One of the most common goals that individuals have in our society is to lose weight. Most fail at this goal for a variety of reasons, but one of the biggest reasons is not focusing on adherence to some very basic strategies. Let's put the following statement into the SMART format. "I want to lose weight."

Specific. We need to hone in and be more specific. "I want to lose ten pounds." Let's agree that while weight loss is good, it can be better if we focus specifically on body fat.

Measurable. There are several different ways that we can measure body fat and overall progress, from highly accurate Bod Pods to fat calipers, or even photographs.

Attainable. We have to ask ourselves whether this goal is realistic within the time constraint or whether there are significant impediments to our goal, such as having a newborn or going on a vacation where we may blow it with unhealthy food choices.

Relevant. Our actions should not only support our goals but also be the most efficient use of our time. While walking is a great activity that we should all do, if we have an hour a day to exercise and are healthy enough to do so, our time might be better spent lifting in the weight room or doing some type of high-intensity conditioning work such as sprints or running stairs/hills.

Time-based. We need to give ourselves a firm but realistic deadline. In this instance, we choose to set our goal at losing fifteen pounds of body fat in four months, which allows for about one pound per week with a little leeway for a vacation, et cetera.

Chunk. To make this fat-loss goal even more effective, we could chunk it down into micro goals. We can have a daily goal of tracking our nutrition app, meeting sleep goals, and having weekly objectives of getting to the gym (and tracking gains).

Action Steps: Identify Your Long-Term Objectives, Supported by Short-Term Goals

1. Identify and write down a specific overarching goal, such as increasing revenue or landing a new job or promotion.
2. Identify and write down at least three supporting goals, and put them in the SMART framework.

CHAPTER 8

BE BRILLIANT ON THE BASICS

In any high-stakes situation you must have the poise, awareness, and presence of mind to read the situation and decide how to act. How quickly and effectively you respond to that decision is based largely on your command of the basics.

SEAL BASICS IN ACTION

Being brilliant on the basics for a SEAL operator means that you practice tactics, drills, and equipment procedures over and over again until you can perform these things at a near-reflexive level. When the pressure is high, you are not thinking about how to use a tactic or how to clear a malfunction in your primary weapons system. Your attention is instead focused on reading the situation, anticipating what comes next, and making the best decision.

The typical urban training known as Special Operations Urban Combat, or SOUC, was three weeks in length and started off at a crawl. Early in the first week of training, after some classroom lessons and walk-throughs on the streets, we would begin patrolling in small elements until the bad guys (role players) would pop out of a window or around a corner and shoot blanks at us. We would execute some very basic drills to maneuver on the enemy or withdraw.

By the end of the third week, we were doing full-blown planned target assaults. Fast-roping out of helos onto rooftops or sneaking through the darkness with night vision goggles and explosively breaching the target buildings while hunting for some specified personnel. Throughout the week we drilled the basics over and over as we layered on more skills and tactics. By the final few scenarios, the instructors were throwing the kitchen sink at us in terms of complexity and confusion. We would have to split up our forces to go after additional bad guys or rescue personnel from a downed helo, all while taking heavy enemy fire and performing realistic medical drills on our wounded.

Oftentimes, especially in the business world, we get stuck chasing the shiny object, the new software, the new methodology for building better communication and collaboration when, really, it's the strong foundation built from a solid mastery of fundamental skills that is critical to our success.

I remember sitting through a class shortly before one of my Iraq deployments. One seasoned and highly respected senior SEAL operator was briefing us on his previous combat deployment and teaching us about the tactics that they had employed. One of the main points he drove home was that in many of the engagements with hardened enemy fighters, it was a reliance on basic infantry tactics that carried the day. Being able to read the terrain, select the right tactic, and perform this tactic faster than the enemy can respond will often be the deciding factor in a combat engagement.

HOW TO BE BRILLIANT ON THE BASICS: PUTTING IN THE WORK

Being brilliant on the basics sounds simple and straightforward . . . and it is. However, it comes with the hard truth that there is no substitute for putting the work in. There are countless examples from Kobe Bryant to Tiger Woods where the athlete spends hours upon hours practicing some of the most fundamental aspects of their craft. These highly successful athletes are often referred to as naturals, or natural shooters. In reality, their success comes at the intersection between talent, hard work with reps, and sets of physical and mental skills.

When a SEAL platoon is overseas engaged in combat operations, they are often moving very fast and often very loose. They are a well-oiled machine. Operators can recognize their teammates in the dark just by the way they walk. They learn to anticipate what that teammate will do and read off them when clearing a compound or house. Their tactics and procedures are very much tuned to that specific environment.

When the SEAL platoon returns, some members will move on to other assignments and new members will be onboarded, but the core of the platoon will remain. The training cycle for the next deployment begins almost immediately. Despite the recent combat experience of the platoon, the tactics are revisited at the most basic and fundamental level. Close-quarter combat-room clearances start off with "two-man room entries." New operators must learn these basics, but all operators are brought back down to the crawl stages and made to perform these basic tactics as cleanly and perfectly as possible. Being too far down "your working wall" during a room clearance gets you a scolding in the debrief. Being close to perfect at very basic procedures develops a solid tactical foundation on which speed and skill progression can be easily developed.

Again, simple and straightforward, but with this comes the understanding that there are no shortcuts and no substitutes for putting the work in. During land warfare and urban combat training blocks, it is customary for SEAL platoons to work fifteen- to eighteen-hour days when training on the road. Much of this work involves kicking in doors, shooting, and blowing things up, all fun stuff. There are also much less glamorous parts of the job that require the same if not more attention.

In Iraq, when driving to an objective in a convoy, as a "ground assault force," we would often leave the gate with ten to fifteen vehicles. This might include our Iraqi partner force and their vehicles if they weren't riding in ours. Getting a large convoy of operators, partner forces, enemy detainees, and casualties to and from a target smoothly is no easy task. Simple? Pretty much, but not easy. It starts with a head count and "ready up" check-in from the rear of the convoy. None of the shiny high-speed equipment or brilliant and innovative tactics are worth a damn if you can't get to and from the objective with all the people you need to leave and return with.

We also spent a lot of time organizing our team and coordinating our movements over radio. Basic radio procedures are practiced over and over to ensure that succinct messages are heard and understood.

In our professional and personal pursuits, it's easy to focus on the shiny new process or equipment. Whether you are into tactical shooting or a sport that involves cutting-edge gear and equipment, you will see the top performers decked out in the latest gear. They have the latest gear because at the highest levels of competition that equipment will give them a fractional advantage. If you were to ask top competitive shooters or tactical shooting instructors where you should spend most of your money . . . on what equipment? Most recommend you spend your time and money on ammo and practice fundamental shooting drills.

The simple fact is that when we want to perform at our best, there is no substitute for putting in the reps and sets. We want to—we need to—hone our craft and develop our abilities to set ourselves apart in the competitive space or to be as effective and engaged in the moments that matter. We must chase and learn advanced skills and processes, but only after we have built the solid foundation of fundamentals. When we consistently drill basics, we get that much closer to mastery, which in turn lets us focus better on the task at hand.

PREPARE TO EXECUTE EFFECTIVELY: DO YOUR RESEARCH

If you are in a job where you directly face a customer or lead a team, you must ensure that you have credibility by being well prepared for whatever engagement or training session you find yourself in. Think about the small details that can be taken care of before this engagement. What client research or industry research can be done? Part of maintaining or presenting credibility in an important moment is driving smoothly through a conversation or presentation and not stumbling on talking points or fumbling with equipment. What can you practice and rehearse to be efficient yet relaxed when in situations that matter? In order to fully leverage and maximize your experiences, what team and individual post-assessment and analysis methods and procedures can you routinely employ?

PRACTICE FOR LIFE ON THE X: PROFESSIONAL BASICS

Here are a few examples of some professional basics for the leader, team, or individual:

1. Gain a firm grasp of the guidance given by leaders as well as the direction of the organization.
2. Distill that guidance and direction into clear action for your team or subordinates. This also applies to solo-preneurs. Your actions must be aligned and support your professional objectives.
3. Plan and rehearse. Before an engagement or call with a client/customer, determine steps to plan and rehearse for maximum readiness. Before meeting with an important client, what type of research have you done on all those in attendance, the organization, and the latest in their industry? What is their current organizational or industry climate? What are their pain points?
4. Develop a game plan for the desired outcome. What is my objective for this engagement versus my long-term/ultimate engagement?
5. Prepare for contingencies. What are a few unplanned things that could unfold?

As simple or obvious a concept as it may seem to focus on being brilliant on the basics, we are never too advanced or developed to lose focus on the fundamentals. We must also reconcile the fact that it will require an investment of time and resources. It's this solid connection to the basics, however, that enables us to build more advanced skills, processes, and procedures.

FOCUS DURING THE BASICS: INVEST IN COGNITIVE REAL ESTATE

When you find yourself on the X and the pressure is on, you need maximum focus on the here and now—what's immediately in front of you? You must be fully engaged and able to read the situation to decide what is best to do and say in that moment. Without fluency in the basics or the ability to lean on some fundamental procedures, you must use some of that cognitive power on less important details and tasks. These details water down your focus and increase your mental load. Despite what you might believe, the research shows that we humans are not effective multitaskers. The fewer things we focus on, the better we will perform. Make every effort to clear the needless distractions by taking care of the easy things. When you accumulate enough of these, your efficiency will drastically improve.

Former NFL player Anthony Trucks learned the importance of being brilliant on the basics while playing Division 1 college football. He understood that come game day, every decision or thought would occupy space in his cognitive real estate. He knew that even high-performance athletes had limited capacity to make timely and highly focused decisions under pressure. The more details and less-important decisions he could take care of in advance, the more focus and confidence he would have during game time. Anthony was machinelike in taking care of his pregame routine. Before a game he knew exactly what his pregame foods would be. When taking the field for the pregame warm-up, he would do only what the coaches and trainers instructed him to do—nothing else. He knew exactly where he could sit in quiet and what mental imagery he would use.

Take care of as many details in advance as possible, maintain your focus, and direct your decision-making on the stuff that matters.

BE A MACHINE

There are basically two types of firearms shooting we do in the SEAL Teams: marksmanship and tactical shooting. Marksmanship is slow and controlled fire from a distance. You take your time and ensure that every shot is achieved with pinpoint accuracy. We use this for basic fundamentals, sniper fire, and sighting in, or zeroing, weapon sights and optics such as scopes or red-dot sights.

Tactical shooting is geared toward placing accurate fire faster and usually at closer ranges, often with multiple targets. As you progress, the speed demands increase while you are shooting on the move, from behind cover, all while reloading and clearing weapons malfunctions. During weapons training on the range, one particular instructor would constantly harp on us to be machinelike in our weapons handling. We would present our weapons to shoot, handle reloads, and scan for threats the exact same way every time. On the rooftop, being shot at for the first time, I was machinelike with my weapons and equipment handling, and that enabled my focus to be applied to the situational awareness and decision-making, instead of the basic skills that I had practiced so many times.

Action Steps: Become Brilliant on the Basics at Work

Being brilliant on the basics is admittedly a broad category but entirely approachable if we break it down to a few very simple components.

1. Prepare your workspace for performance and focus. When preparing for routine and repeated events or high-stakes situations, what are three to five very basic things that you do the same way every time? How can you be machinelike in preparing your virtual setup or workspace? Can you set up at least fifteen minutes early and run through a checklist ensuring that everything is dialed in?

2. Develop a research routine. Before an important engagement, what research or study methods can you make a habit?

3. Plan for contingencies. What happens when your laptop unexpectedly reboots, or you have some other technical glitch—what will you do? What potential direction could a pitch, team meeting, or client engagement take?

4. What lessons can you take away from repeatable events? Whether it's for your team or for you as the individual performer, develop a framework or checklist that can be used to gather the lessons learned and to feed those lessons into action steps in preparing for the next event.

CHAPTER 9

MENTAL SKILLS: MANAGE ENERGY AND FOCUS

In order to fully optimize a SEAL's performance in combat, instructors and command psychologists employ performance psychology techniques that have helped elite athletes handle the pressure of competition for years.

When creating and teaching the Warrior Toughness Program, the performance psychology part of the curriculum centered around these basic areas: tactical breathing, mental rehearsal, goal-setting, energy management, and self-talk. Years prior to the WTP, many of these techniques were adapted and used to great effect at BUD/S training at the Naval Special Warfare Center in Coronado, California. Prior to this training, many otherwise-good SEAL candidates were failing to get through the most stressful and mentally demanding tests in the program.

UNDERWATER AND UNDER PRESSURE: USING MENTAL SKILLS TO SUCCEED

Historically, BUD/S training has an attrition rate ranging from 75 to 90 percent. The one part of training that weeds out the most candidates is known as Hell Week. Hell Week is also the most famous part of training due to its sheer brutality and dramatic images of exhausted candidates carrying boats and logs while covered in mud and sand. Hell Week is often moved around a bit but is currently five days of suffering in the middle of First Phase of BUD/S.

Throughout the week, the trainees are run nonstop and given only a few short sleep breaks. When not conducting grueling team exercises, trainees are immersed in the cold water of the Pacific Ocean until hypothermic. This training is about the individual proving to the instructor staff, his team, and most of all himself that he can go well past preconceived limits, or what his body is telling him. He must prove that he is willing to put the needs of the mission and his teammates above his own personal suffering.[2] Candidates who successfully complete Hell Week, and the other testable requirements of First Phase, move on to Second Phase (Dive Phase). Dive Phase is where the candidates face their second major hurdle to graduation with a test known as pool competency, or pool comp.

Pool comp is the culmination of a five-day pool week where candidates are taught basic scuba diving techniques in a nine-foot swimming pool. Starting with a very rudimentary familiarization of scuba, you progress to where you are taking your scuba tank off and putting it on your buddy and vice versa. You take your gear on and off underwater in precise order, and you even do it with a blacked-out face mask to simulate nighttime conditions. You run through daily tests, and if there's any deviation from the correct sequence, you fail the test. If you fail the retest, you are sent back in training or dropped if deemed an unsuitable candidate.

Day five is the actual day for pool comp. This test finds the candidate swimming along the bottom of the pool. The instructors attack, ripping your mask and fins off, and begin to introduce increasingly more difficult interruptions to your air source. The dual-hose breathing regulator is taken from your mouth and then wrapped around your air tank or tied in knots.

When the instructors have finished creating this series of obstacles,

---

2.　BUD/S training is open to women, but as of this writing, none have been selected to attend training yet.

the candidate must calmly go through a gradual sequence of trying to solve the problem. This starts with trying to undo the knot or fix other problems with the tank on your back and then ditching the scuba gear, if required, in the exact order to untie the knot, et cetera. After going through this process several times, you become starved for air. You feel the instinctive urge to bolt to the surface. If that urge takes over and becomes the dominant thought, then you lose your focus on the sequence and procedure that will get you through the situation with success. When this happens, it is likely that you will either panic and bolt to the surface or you will perform something incorrectly or out of sequence. In either event you fail the test, or evolution, as it's called.

The SEAL Teams need individuals who can keep pushing on and fighting when injured or against overwhelming odds. One BUD/S instructor told us that no matter how cold or miserable we were at BUD/S, life in the Teams would be harder. I certainly found this to be true. Hell Week is highly effective in testing the candidates' mental and physical toughness as well as their ultimate commitment. Pool comp, on the other hand, tests your ability to problem-solve and remain calm while solving scuba problems, but it fundamentally tests how you can generally resist panic and stay focused on the behaviors and actions that will bring success in high-pressure situations.

TACTICAL BREATHING: ENERGY MANAGEMENT AND FOCUS

Situational skills and self-efficacy, or belief in self, are essential, but we help manage the physiology side of the house with some very useful breathing techniques.

Breathing techniques for performance have been around for thousands of years, but only more recently have we, at least in the West, begun to adopt them for a variety of contexts and environments.

Sometimes referred to as box breathing, this specific manner of breathing can be highly effective in lowering the arousal energy—especially fear, anger, and frustration—and enabling the performer to focus on the present and execute successfully.

WARRIOR TOUGHNESS BREATHING: RECALIBRATE

Warrior Toughness training teaches a version of tactical breathing that we refer to as "recalibrating." In order to recalibrate, recruits are trained in this practice as follows:

- Exhale all your breath.
- Slowly inhale, counting to six.
- Hold at the top of your inhale for a count of two.
- Exhale with control for a count of seven.
- Hold at the bottom of the exhale for a count of two.
- Repeat.

Recruits are often taught to use imagery such as drawing an imaginary square while breathing. Inhale is the first vertical line, exhale is first horizontal line, and so forth. This is an easy introduction to using mindfulness in their breathing exercises.

In my own experience in teaching this technique, many have found that the count is a bit too long. When using tactical breathing techniques, the count is far less important than that the breathing be slow and controlled and done inhaling through the nose, filling the diaphragm and the lungs, and then exhaling slowly through the mouth.

To offer up an example, Seaman Recruit Sanchez, a young Navy recruit, has been at Recruit Training Command, or Navy Boot Camp, for several weeks. She has been drinking through a fire hose of information, is short on sleep, and is missing home. She finds herself as lead nozzle operator during a high-stress firefighting training event. She is trying to fight the fire—to remember the procedures all while being yelled at by instructors. She is stressed and overwhelmed, causing her to lock up and freeze. She cannot think clearly, and in this scenario any training value becomes lost.

The old way of training this recruit would be to continue yelling at her, thinking she needed further motivation or that the added stress would aid in the training value with increased stress inoculation.

However, research suggests that stress inoculation (being better prepared to perform in future stressful events) is only effective if that person has made an adaptation based on that stressful event. Without teaching deliberate coping methods, there is no assurance that that sailor will perform better next time.

During most combat-style military training, including firefighting, the intent is to ramp the stress up as much as safely and realistically possible to prepare the trainees for the often near-crippling effects of exposure to the real thing. The expert military trainer will facilitate and lead challenging and stressful events that push the trainee to the brink of what they can handle in terms of physical and mental stress, but they will pull back just short of the limit. The trainer wants the trainee to feel as much realism as possible, but if at a certain point the trainee can no longer perform the training sequences, then there is no point in going further because doing so could be catastrophic under certain high-risk training conditions.

Under the Warrior Toughness Program at Navy Boot Camp, this young, overwhelmed recruit will be ordered to recalibrate. When the recruit is given this command, she knows to stop and close her eyes or maintain a soft focus in front of her. She will begin diaphragmatic breathing by inhaling through her nose for a count of six seconds. She will hold her breath for two seconds and exhale through her mouth for seven seconds. She will then hold her breath for two seconds and repeat the sequence. After several of these breaths, she will be told to repeat the basic procedures, sequences, and responsibilities that will lead to success. After that she will reengage, and the data suggests that 90 percent of the time she will be successful. We don't send people into fires or gunfights without the specific technical and physical skills, so we are failing them if we don't train them with the necessary mental skills to perform under pressure.

BREATHING IN CRISIS

Six months later, aboard the USS *McFaul*, the alarm for general quarters and battle stations sounds. It is 3:00 a.m. and Seaman Sanchez is roused from her sleep. The *McFaul* has just taken a missile hit with unknown damage and casualties. Sanchez knows instantly what she must do. She quickly makes her way to the repair locker, where she will don her firefighting gear, and with her fire party she will go save the ship.

As she makes her way down the noisy passageway, she is aware of the symptoms of fear. She arrives at the compartment and begins getting her gear on while listening to the damage control report.

She will be going into the heart of the fire. She notices her hands are sweating and her heart is racing. She begins to feel light-headed. "Recalibrate, Sanchez!" she tells herself. While she is getting her fire-fighting equipment and respirator on, she begins to control her breath. She feels fear but it does not grab hold of her. As she feels herself calm down, she begins to focus on how she needs to engage; she thinks of the sequences and procedures that she needs to execute to be an effective part of the firefighting team and save the ship.

Mindfulness training is used by not only soldiers and athletes but also top leaders and performers in the business world. Andrew Swinand is the CEO of Publicis Groupe Creative and Production US and CEO of Leo Burnett Worldwide, an advertising company. Andrew realizes that in frantic and stressful business environments, managing energy is critical. "You need to teach people about the energy you bring to a situation. Managing energy in business situations is like marksmanship shooting: if you are out of breath and not focused, you are not going to hit your target. With that analogy in mind, take control of your breathing and focus your mind so that when you walk into a room with positive energy and intention, the team will follow."

Knowing your stuff—being brilliant on the basics—when paired with controlled breathing techniques will be the essential first steps to get yourself centered and focused when you feel like emotions and distractions may derail you.

MENTAL REHEARSAL

Whether we are pitching a client or the C-suite, or presenting to the team we are leading, we want to spend the time preparing and rehearsing for that moment. We can harness the power of mental rehearsal by putting ourselves in that room well before the event.

Many of us who came up in the Teams and had successful careers—before mental training was a thing—intuitively used mental strategies based on what we felt would be useful before going into high-pressure situations.

As a new guy in my first platoon, I wasn't a rock star the first time I tried close-quarters combat. I became so fixated on the footwork aspect of entering a room: how far away my feet were from the wall, how far down the wall I traveled, and so forth. These were a couple of the things that the instructors really harped on, and strangely, it gave me some trouble. One exasperated instructor remarked, "Drum, I never thought I would have to say this, but tonight when we are finished, I just want you to practice walking through a door." He was probably half-serious. Eventually I became decent at this skill because I learned how to mentally rehearse what the situation or room would look like while I waited for my turn. If the guy in front of me moved to the left, I went right. I would sweep, looking for targets, and the targets would be shoot or no shoot, depending on what's in their hands. We would come to the next door, and that door enters into a hallway. If I have a closed door on the left, adjacent to an open door on the right, what do I do?

Years later, as a tactical leader I would use this strategy while riding on helos or in trucks on the way to an objective for assault. We always built in what-ifs, or contingencies, for every phase of the operation. I would review these contingencies in my mind. What if a helicopter breaks before we even take off? What if we have a minimum force plan, meaning we have enough operators to accomplish the mission, but who will stay behind and who will go? Where will I put them? What if a helicopter gets shot down? What if while patrolling into the target area we become compromised or enter a gunfight before we get there and lose the element of surprise?

Sanchez Rehearses

Sanchez starts to think about what is next . . . where she is going with the fire party. The fire is in the aft engineering spaces in the rear of the ship. She is familiar with the area and starts to visualize what the space will look like with a fire raging. What will she see? What will the heat feel like? What noises will she hear and what will she smell?

Sanchez is using imagery to put herself in the situation ahead of time. She is painting a vivid picture for herself to help her effectively mentally rehearse what she is about to face. She is visualizing herself performing the basic tasks and sequences successfully. When she is finished with that, she is thinking about obstacles that she might face. She is thinking about the things that could deviate from the plan and challenge her, but again she will visualize herself performing her tasks correctly and successfully.

Seaman Sanchez is using some very fundamental performance psychology techniques to mentally prepare herself for success when she walks onto the X.

VISUALIZATION

We use our senses to aid in our visualization to make the scenario as realistic and vivid as possible. We can also use various "camera lenses" to see ourselves perform.

If you ever watch the Olympics and happen to get a glimpse of an athlete's pre-event routine, you might see them doing a strange little dance with their eyes closed as they move through their routine or performance sequence in their mind. There is no more dramatic or effective example of this technique than that of high diver Laura Wilkinson's 2000 Olympics performance.

Six months prior to those Olympic Games, Wilkinson broke her foot during one of the higher-risk routines. As the games approached, she was unable to practice any of her dives. Instead, she would climb the thirty-three-foot platform, close her eyes, and mentally rehearse her various routines. Her focus and discipline in employing this tactic landed her in eighth place in the preliminaries, enabling her to make it to the finals. She went on to win gold despite the inability to train and physically practice her dives. She credited visualization with her gold medal–winning performance.

SELF-TALK

We humans talk to ourselves more than we do to anyone else in each day, but the inner dialogues can often be destructive and self-defeating. We often fill our heads with negative thoughts without understanding the power that our thoughts have in shaping our emotions and behavior. Negative thoughts can prevent us from focusing on the drive to a successful performance or engagement. In contrast, self-talk can be used to guide us with confidence and focus through our high-stakes moments.

Self-Talk to Gold: Dana Vollmer's Comeback

Dana Vollmer is one of the US's most highly decorated Olympic swimmers. Her path was not without its challenges and setbacks, however. Vollmer won her first Olympic gold medal in the 2004 Summer Olympics in Athens. She was sixteen years old. After she failed to qualify for the 2008 games, it hit her hard—she was having a difficult time dealing with the pressure of meeting expectations and trying to elevate her performance as a swimmer. Failing to make the 2008 team caused her to do some significant soul-searching and self-evaluation. During practice she would find her mind racing through all the things she had to do well and what to avoid doing. This inner dialogue was detracting from her performance. Out of the pool she also had a hard time dealing with the pressure. She needed to better control the dialogue in her mind if she was to get back on track as an athlete and live a more balanced and fulfilled life.

In order to combat the negative thoughts and scripts, she knew she had to improve her self-talk. Dana found a way to effectively combine imagery with a self-talk dialogue that served her.

To manage the pressure, Dana would often tell herself, "Little by little, get better at something every day." Dana knew that amazing world-class performances are, in fact, outliers. Rather than focusing on those outlier moments and attaining perfection, she reduced the pressure by more effectively focusing on raising her average performances, which would in turn lead to an overall improvement. The outlier and amazing races would now be faster. She told herself that "there is no such thing as a bad race as long as I learned something."

Dana went on to smash records and win more gold medals, and she was one of the first Olympic swimmers to successfully compete as a mom! She finished a successful racing career, retiring on her terms, and currently uses and teaches what she learned in the business world.

Action Steps: Cultivating Your Energy-Management Skills

You have identified your high-stakes moments in the previous chapters' actions steps. Pick one particular moment. Then take that experience through these three techniques:

1. Tactical/recalibrate breathing. Create a space and time to practice your controlled breathing before walking onto the X. Identify what situations might distress or heighten levels of energy or arousal. Be ready to use the recalibrate technique to lower that arousal or tune out distractions when needed. You can begin to familiarize yourself with this tactical breathing by practicing the following way:

    •   Find a quiet spot free of distraction to sit comfortably. Close your eyes or gaze softly at the floor or wall in front of you.
    •   Inhale through your nose for a count of five seconds. Focus on filling your diaphragm (upper belly) and then your lungs.
    •   Pause and hold for two seconds.
    •   Exhale through your mouth for a count of six seconds.
    •   Pause and hold for two seconds and repeat.
    •   Once you get the hang of this, you can stop counting the length of breaths and focus on the rising and falling of your chest and belly, or the feeling of the clothing against your skin. Remember that when doing breathing and mindfulness training, it is less about the count and more about being present in the here and now.
    •   While you are breathing, try adding other mindfulness components such as imagery. You can picture your breath flickering a flame on a candle a few feet in

front of you. Feel the weight of your body in the chair, the weight of your hands and arms on your legs, or the feeling of your feet on the floor.

With practice, this will be a technique that you can use on the fly. And it will be a tool that comes to mind when you are feeling stress, anger, or distraction. You can do it while driving or sitting outside or walking into an important situation.

Pro tip: I often find it helpful to unwind after a busy day by lying in bed and doing three sets of counting my exhalation breaths from one to ten. If you get distracted and lose count, start over at one.

2. Mental rehearsal/visualization. Mentally rehearse the moment you are preparing for. Look at yourself through a camera view. One that sees what you would see and one that sees you as if you were on a TV screen. See yourself performing the sequences exactly as you practiced. Imagine yourself feeling calm and composed and then executing with precision. Use your senses to visualize what you see, feel, and hear. In an office setting it might be the clicking of pens, the smell of coffee, et cetera.

3. Self-talk. It must be specific, realistic, and most of all helpful. It's good to say "I got this," but it's even more effective to drill down to something more specific. Remind yourself of what you have practiced and reviewed, and what you know. There may be certain things you want to maintain your focus on during an event. Write those down and repeat them to ensure your actions and thoughts are guided toward them.

CHAPTER 10

MINDFULNESS TRAINING

Have you ever gotten in your car after a long day at work and turned the key or pushed the Start button and the next thing you know you are home in your driveway? It's as if the magic car has just transported you home.

Mindfulness is defined as our ability to stay present in the here and now. When acting mindfully, we are not thinking about the past or engaged in daydreaming about the future. In a high-stakes moment we are not thinking about the consequences of a poor performance or negative outcome. We are fully engaged and focused on what is happening right now. We may notice distractions around us or our own thoughts and feelings, but we do not get carried away by them. When we are mindful, we are observing in a nonjudgmental way.

One of my psychologist partners used the analogy that mindfulness training is like bodybuilding for the brain. A bicep curl exertion includes lifting the weight, the *concentric* muscle movement, and lowering the weight, the *eccentric* motion associated with that movement. When we get distracted and pull our focus back to the exercise or activity in a nonjudgmental manner, this act is similar to how we lift and lower weights. The act of being distracted and returning to focus strengthens the frontal cortex in the brain, creating new pathways.

There are many researched and documented benefits to meditation, and its increase in popularity in the Western world is for good reason. Anecdotally, meditation has made a huge difference in my life, increasing both my performance and the quality of my relationships through self-regulation and emotional control. Meditation can help with stress management, mental recovery, and athletic performance, as well as improving the quality of sleep.

WARRIOR TOUGHNESS MEDITATION TRAINING: BREATH WORK, MENTAL AND BODY SCANS

When exploring how to make our Navy sailors tougher, we knew we needed women and men that could perform under pressure, deal with the daily and prolonged grind, and take a hit and keep going. Meditation, or mindfulness training, as we called it, was one of the primary tools that we used to develop much of this capacity.

We wanted our sailors to have increased focus during stressful times and when in a state of fatigue. We wanted them to have the emotional awareness that would lead to emotional control. Lastly, we wanted them to have the skills to recover mentally and physically after stressful events.

When we introduced mindfulness training to our new Navy students, the psychologists would ask if they knew how long Buddhist monks, some of the most dedicated meditators, could keep their minds free of thoughts. Most were quite surprised to learn that the average time monks could be free of thoughts was around twelve seconds! Again, it is the practice of getting distracted and bringing awareness back that strengthens the frontal cortex of the brain.

The Warrior Toughness Program team of psychologists developed a meditation curriculum for training. The first few exercises focused mostly on breathing, with a bit of imagery or visualization to give the recruits additional things to focus on. Breathing is such a key component to mindfulness not only because of the physiological effects but also because it is an easy thing to focus on when distracted or emotionally hijacked. As my friend and psychologist colleague would say, "You can only breathe in the present, you can't breathe for yesterday and you can't breathe for tomorrow." Over the course of several weeks, the recruits learned more progressive techniques, such as the mental and body scan and muscle relaxation.

The mental scan involves observing thoughts as they pass before you as if on a conveyor belt or on a leaf floating downstream. The body scan entails scanning up and down the body while resting the focus on specific areas for a few moments.

Progressive muscle relaxation is a great tool that is used for relaxation and recovery. Typically starting from one end of the body, the muscles are tensed for about ten seconds before relaxing. Each muscle group is tensed and relaxed multiple times. Done effectively, this will increase mind-body awareness while enabling a deep state of relaxation.

MINDFULLY TRIGGERING THE AUTOPILOT TOGGLE SWITCH: SUCCESSFUL SEQUENCING

One of the most fundamental weapons-handling skills that SEAL operators are taught in close-quarter combat (CQC) is the weapons transition drill. When your primary weapon, typically a short-barrel rifle, or carbine, goes click because of a malfunction or the magazine runs dry of ammunition, then the immediate action sequence is to drop your carbine, still attached to its sling, and immediately draw your pistol. Because theoretically the threat is so close, there is no time to do anything else. When fighting in an urban setting, you may be engaged in CQC but also find yourself in the middle of a street fight. In this situation, the threat may be much farther away, and going to your pistol when your carbine runs empty will likely not be the best option. Instead, taking a knee behind cover and clearing the malfunction or reloading your carbine makes much more sense. Whether transitioning to a pistol or reloading the carbine, these things happen reflexively or while on autopilot.

The key distinguishing factor here is that one must have the situational presence and awareness to choose the proper sequence. Being present for sharp decision-making and then switching to autopilot for well-practiced automatic sequences is key for combat-related or high-stress tasks. It is as if every choice or decision in a combat or high-stakes situation is represented on a large Italian restaurant menu. You deliberately and intentionally select a menu item that best serves the situation and then the trained reflexes take over.

MINDFULNESS TRAINING: THE BENEFITS TO YOU

Meditating and mindfulness require discipline and dedication, like running and going to the gym. You must practice consistently to reap the benefits. As with the gym, results will take some time, but I feel strongly that it is worth the investment. Benefits to training your brain include

- **Stress management.** When we feel elevated levels of stress, we tend to carry that stress with us moving forward if we are not deliberate about bringing ourselves back down to baseline. Mindfulness training with techniques like progressive muscle relaxation is effective in returning us to our calm state.
- **Emotional awareness and regulation.** The more we meditate, the more we become aware of our thoughts and physical sensations. When we are aware of our feelings of anger, fear, and anxiety, we can choose to interrupt a potential emotional hijacking by reframing our thoughts and choosing an alternate behavior.
- **Focus.** The practice of getting distracted and gently bringing the mind back to awareness repeatedly will help sharpen your focus in the face of distractions.

The purpose of this book is not to teach you meditation or mindfulness—there are plenty of other resources for that. My purpose here is to show you how this can be part of an overall process and routine. I want you to make it an important part of how you prepare to be at your best.

But I do need to highlight one very important point here. Despite the many benefits that mindfulness training provides to most, it is not for everyone. Mindfulness training or meditation can trigger distress and other unwanted side effects in certain individuals. For those who have suffered severe emotional trauma or experience mental struggles, I strongly urge you to receive guidance from a mental health professional before beginning mindfulness training.

MINDFULNESS IN DAILY LIFE

When we put in the work of practicing and rehearsing, we can feel confident in anticipation of our "On the X" moment. When we train mindfully, we can execute these skills with situational presence and awareness required for optimum performance.

When I step out onstage or take the front of the room for a keynote or workshop presentation, I am not thinking intensely about what is going to come out of my mouth . . . that will come mostly from autopilot because of the hours I spent rehearsing. When I take the stage, I am instead focusing on connecting with the audience or scanning to ensure that everything is working as it should. I am effectively toggling between mindfulness and autopilot.

Obviously, I am not a psychologist or a mindfulness expert but feel that there is great value in hearing from an end user and beneficiary of these different techniques. In my life I tend to typically go for the simplest approach. When it comes to mindfulness, there are a few ways that I personally use it as a tool or exercise:

1. **Smartphone app.** There are many good ones out there—I happen to use Headspace. I will usually do ten to fifteen minutes a day.
2. **Activity mindfulness.** I will often apply mindfulness when I am on a walk or when driving. While I am walking, I am looking around, observing colors, smells, temperatures, et cetera.
3. **Driving mindfully.** When I am driving, I will take a few moments to scan the road, reading signs, license plates, observing cars and pedestrians, practicing observing what's going on while resisting the effort to get carried away on autopilot.

Action Steps: Meditating with Self-Compassion and Consistency

It is important to note that we are going to be constantly distracted and carried away mentally when we practice mindfulness or meditation. The more we practice, as with everything, the better we become. Try this:

1. Pick one of these activities to focus on. And when your mind wanders, gently and without judgment bring the focus back.

    •   Tooth brushing. While brushing your teeth, focus only on the act of brushing and how the bristles feel on your teeth as well as any other sensations.
    •   Eating. During a meal, bring your attention to the experience. Focus on chewing. Notice the smell, texture, and flavor of the food.
    •   Movement. While mindfully driving or walking, focus on exactly what you see, feel, hear, and smell.
    •   Prayer. If devotion is a part of your life, bring awareness to it. Notice if it drifts away from the prayer and return to the words and the feeling of spirit in your body.

2. Select one method for guided meditation, and commit to daily practice. Start small and work your way up until it becomes a habit. There are great smartphone apps that you can use (Headspace, Insight Timer, Calm, Ten Percent Happier), and you can even find some guided meditations on YouTube.

If you are curious about your level of readiness for your next on the X opportunity, I have designed the High-Stakes Preparedness Assessment. You can take the assessment free on my website at stephendrum.com.

Part 3

COMMIT

REFLECT PREPARE

EXECUTE

When it comes to execution, we must reconcile the fact that so much of the result, or outcome, is beyond our control. When I talk about performing and *succeeding* on the X, what I am really referring to are the things that *you* control. We can't control the actions of clients or teammates, but we do control how we prepare, deliver, and respond to curveballs. Because you are a professional, and because of what you have learned in this book, you understand the need to prioritize proper preparation for your important moments. You have done the market and client research; you have rehearsed your presentation. You have earned a robust performance statement that acknowledges the work you have put in. Before I take the stage to deliver an important keynote speech, I feel the pressure and the nerves but also acknowledge to myself all the things that I have done to prepare and enable my success.

Of all the skills and mission sets in military special operations, combat diving is, in my opinion, the most difficult. It may not be the most exhausting, painful, or dangerous, but it requires extraordinary planning and skill to be successful.

On a night-dive in Key West I remember looking up at a pier light on the surface and seeing the silhouette of a very large shark pass over me. As a SEAL there are many opportunities to feel fear, but one's concern for their professional reputation and dedication to mission success override much of it. In the case of combat diving, the required focus is so intense that it will take front and center over the fear of such things as sharks swimming around you in the darkness.

Still, being completely lost underwater in a harbor has made for some of the most frustrating experiences of my life. Almost every SEAL has a story of how their dive pair was terribly lost and the driver (navigator of the buddy pair) was so exasperated that he thrust his navigation attack board at the buddy, indicating for him to take over the navigation portion of the dive. The buddy usually pushes the attack board back, since he has no better clue on how to proceed. Surfacing to get a look around is not an option as you risk not only your life but also the other dive pairs in the water. It definitely makes for some funny stories at the post-mission debrief. With enough luck and composure, the pair can recover the dive by moving in squares until they can find something familiar from the mission-planning harbor study.

In life, when doing things that matter, you often don't know how well you are prepared until things go wrong. I would venture to say that every SEAL has had dives that have gone wrong. In a training environment, worst case is a diving medical emergency, while the best case is you fail a training dive and suffer humiliation and embarrassment in front of peers and instructor staff.

The mark of any true professional in any field is the lengths to which they are willing to go to ensure that they are prepared for any contingency. In this part of the book I share a system that you can apply to your own performance strategy—one that builds in rehearsal, contingency planning, awareness, and agility—that functions as an insurance policy on your actions.

CHAPTER 11

REHEARSAL

San Clemente Island is twenty-one nautical miles long and sits approximately sixty miles west of the San Diego coastline. This island plays host to Third Phase of BUD/S training, which is the final hurdle for SEAL trainees before graduation. The primary focus for Third Phase is all things related to land warfare: weapons, explosives, tactics, and mission planning. It's during this training that SEAL trainees get their first exposure to mission planning, briefing, and rehearsals. After the mission brief, known as the operations order, walk-throughs and rehearsals are conducted. It is literally make-believe time. For rehearsal, whatever props, military vehicles, and buildings are available are used to simulate structures or terrain features that might be at the objective. Small but important details such as where you are sitting in a helo or vehicle are gone over, ensuring all participants are on the same page.

COMBAT SWIMMER

I previously mentioned how combat diving or being a combat swimmer, as the role is referred to in the Teams, is one of the most difficult skill sets or missions to complete successfully. Here is why.

Combat swimmer missions are done not on the scuba gear that civilians use but instead with the use of rebreathers. This closed-circuit system recycles pure oxygen through a canister that cleanses toxic levels of CO_2 from the exhalation breath. This system allows for quiet operation and no bubbles in order to avoid detection by those that may be on the surface. Mastering these devices requires hours upon hours of practice.

A complete mission, or full mission profile, as it is called, may involve casting dive pairs from a boat or helicopter far away from the objective. This typically requires surface swimming for an hour or two before descending into a dive profile at a predetermined point.

Most dives are done in pairs and are conducted in the pitch-black at night. The pair is attached by a nylon rope to avoid separation, since most times it is too dark to see your dive buddy more than a foot away at best. The only tools used to guide the divers to their target are a large compass, a stopwatch, a depth gauge on a plastic board known as the attack board, carried by the driver, and a stopwatch timer used by the buddy. The dive pair has practiced their pace together over and over for several days, meaning that for every kick or minute they swim, they know exactly how far they are traveling. The driver's eyes are glued to the compass and depth gauge to ensure proper course and depth of the dive.

Mission success in this environment means traveling thousands of yards underwater, across harbor channels and through piers, and navigating around other vessels before accurately hitting your target. During mission planning you must account for currents and factor that into your compass bearing. The target itself may be a particular vessel surrounded by dozens of other vessels. You must sort your way through piers and docks that all look the same. Coming up to the surface to look around is not an option. Guards and swimmer detection devices provide extreme hazards to the divers and the mission.

Accomplishing your mission and getting to the extraction point to be picked up without being detected is extremely difficult. On training dives, it was often bragging rights or a point of pride to be one of the first dive pairs to arrive at the extraction point after a successful dive. When on combat swimmer training trips, the last week of training usually consisted of a day-dive with a break, followed by a night-dive.

All told, surface and underwater swimming amounted to dives typically lasting four to five hours.

After the night-dives you're extremely exhausted and suffering with the accumulated illnesses and diving-related issues related to ears, sinuses, open wounds, and ankle overuse. There are plenty of SEALs, myself included, who don't even really like the water. I'm sure you are wondering why the hell we chose this profession! In my defense, I didn't realize this until attaining a level of intimacy with the water that the Teams gave me. By the end of a long dive trip, guys are usually dreading these night-dives, especially in cold water.

Because of the inherent difficulty, suffering, and discomfort involved, successful dives (especially when done faster than the other pairs tasked with the same mission) made for some of the most professionally satisfying experiences in my career.

Successful combat divers are brilliant on the basics. They have their pace down, and they've kept detailed dive logs to know exactly how much buoyancy or weight must be added to be completely neutral in the water—they won't sink or float. The dive pair has researched tides and current studies and planned their navigation route to the target based on current speed and direction. The pair has memorized the harbor charts for distinguishing features and any available intelligence photos to know what the target and surrounding vessels look like. In short, they are prepared to risk their lives for the mission.

REHEARSAL: THE DIRT DIVE

After all the research and brilliance on the basics, there's one key element of execution that remains: rehearsal. Dive pairs will literally walk the dive in the parking lot and simulate and talk through every phase of the dive. They will actually use the attack board and get on an actual compass bearing to help memorize the different headings they will need to take. They will talk through getting to the target and discuss what they will see and hear. The pair will also discuss contingencies and what happens then and what they will see if they end up too far right or left of the target objective or reset point.

Even on land-based targets, walk-through rehearsals with

contingencies are almost always done when the time allows. Making it a habit to put yourself into a challenging situation beforehand is extremely beneficial; it's what top performers in all professions do to be at their best.

Complex, high-stakes moments may require the full Monty of rehearsing every aspect of the event or engagement, including logistics, talking points, contingencies, and other details. Even for low-consequence or more-routine engagements, putting yourself into a situation beforehand is a highly recommended habit. Once you have identified the objectives for an engagement, break it down into phases and figure out how you will practice and rehearse for confidence and sharpness in execution.

Taking the stage as a professional speaker is not that dissimilar from being an athlete or a SEAL as you might think, when it comes to performing on the X. The stakes are high for that speaker; their livelihood depends on their successful execution. Others, such as the event planner or organizational leaders, have placed their trust in the speaker. You will often hear people discuss wanting to avoid over-preparing or over-rehearsing for fear of being too robotic or mechanical. While I never suggest pushing past one's ability to focus, I think this concern is mostly overblown. Most people are simply not rehearsing properly rather than doing too much.

At Heroic Public Speaking, Michael and Amy Port teach what is known as the seven-step rehearsal protocol. This process is extremely detailed and comprehensive, covering every facet of what it takes to rehearse, make adjustments, and ultimately deliver a world-class speech.

1. **Table reads.** The speech script is read aloud, to ensure proper flow and wording, and to start getting more familiar with the script.
2. **Content mapping.** Pauses or beats and operative words are notated.
3. **Blocking and staging.** Just as a theater performer's movements are precisely choreographed, so are the speaker's. All movements are intentional and help with memorization.

4. **Improvisation and rewriting.** Here adjustments are made for speech customization or enhancement. There may be spots that are intentionally left loose for improvisation.
5. **Invited rehearsal.** Key individuals are invited to this rehearsal in order to give very targeted and precise feedback.
6. **Open rehearsal.** This rehearsal is intended to replicate better what the actual speech will look like in terms of a larger audience and logistics.
7. **Dress/tech rehearsal.** Just like wearing your combat gear when you train, microphone and clothing are tested together. Movement in footwear is tested and practiced.

Think back to when we talked about preparing by being brilliant on the basics. When a performer, speaker, or SEAL trains, practices, and rehearses effectively, they hope to achieve what athletes often refer to as a flow state. They know their movements, tactics, and material so well that they don't have to think about what comes next, it flows right out of them. It is not robotic because it is so familiar. When you have this level of preparation, you are more attuned to the environment, able to connect better with those around you, and more prepared to pivot and make adjustments.

You might not be taking the stage as a pro speaker, but if the stakes are high enough, your chances for success are often directly proportional to how well practiced and rehearsed you are. Be disciplined and thorough!

SELF-TALK: THE PERFORMANCE STATEMENT

In chapter 9, I introduced the general concept of self-talk as a mental skill. More specifically, how often the dialogue in our minds can be destructive if we aren't mindful. We must take control of this dialogue when we reflect on our life in general as well as when it comes to preparing for and executing on the X. Our performance during difficult or stressful events can be optimized by what psychologists call the performance statement, or mantra. This mantra is not just a statement of positive or Pollyannish thoughts. It is focused more on the details of performance. I saw this used to great effect by my psychologist colleagues in the Warrior Toughness Program. They taught that a performance statement must be specific and realistic, but most of all helpful. As an example, they would teach the recruits how to improve run times by focusing not on their time, but rather on their stride, breathing, and performing at the best level they are capable of on that day.

A mantra that we use in the SEAL Teams when it comes to describing the most fundamental actions to be taken in a gunfight is "Shoot, move, and communicate!" First, you must return or deliver accurate fire on the enemy. Second, in most cases you will not be fighting from a static position; you will either be maneuvering to crush the enemy or withdrawing from an enemy with the tactical advantage. Lastly, all circumstances, such as the enemy position and maneuver plan, must be called out and communicated to the other team members. Everyone must be on the same page.

In the first part of the book, I shared the story of my first time under fire on a rooftop in Iraq. Though I didn't know it at the time, I was using this mantra as a performance statement. I was telling myself to "shoot, move, communicate." To be clear, there are about a thousand other things that one could think about when in a gunfight on a military battlefield. The point of repeating these three words to myself is that it kept my focus centered on the here and now. It prevented me from thinking about being wounded, killed, or, more importantly, making a bad decision that risked the lives of others.

In the "Mental Skills" chapter, I discussed just how powerful our thoughts are in positively or negatively affecting our emotions and behaviors. When performing on the X and feeling the pressure, or even in other situations where we face distractions, it is easy for our focus to be diverted from the present. If we don't manage our self-talk, then our minds can be easily filled with thoughts that undermine confidence and focus. Our minds start leaping ahead to the consequences of failure or how stupid we may look to others. Crafting an effective performance statement and using it before you walk onto that X will significantly aid in maintaining confidence and focus on where it needs to be.

When I remind myself through a performance statement that I am fully prepared to execute at a high level regardless of the curveballs that get thrown at me, I feel more confident and more relaxed. Just like a professional athlete or SEAL operator, the more confident and relaxed I am, the better I will perform. Here are statements that I might make to allow myself to take the stage with confidence and focus:

"You have trained hard for this talk. You are ready for the curveballs."

"Contrast and stay planted." (These are my cues to contrast the delivery of my words and only use intentional movements.)

"You are so lucky to do what you love."

"You got this! You own this!"

The words you use are not critical; they are simply used to manage energy or center your focus where it needs to be. Remember the mantra that MLB vet Michael Cuddyer used most of his life: "I'm a pro." While this was a great mantra and mission statement, Michael learned later in his career how to effectively use a targeted performance statement to maintain confidence and focus on the field or getting ready to bat. "I am the best player on the field! I put the work in and deserve the same success as the superstars." Talking with Michael in person, he comes across as a very humble guy, but to compete at that level as long as he did, one needs a strong belief in self. It must be said that these are not Pollyannish BS statements that we were told to tell ourselves as kids. In order for this to be effective we have to believe it—we have to earn it. Michael earned his performance statement by putting the work in and believed in his abilities. Remember, we use the performance statement for earned confidence and to keep our focus centered on the task at hand.

Before your big moment, what have you done to be ready—how have you prepared? What curveballs might you face and how? After thoughtful consideration, what are a few performance cues that you may use?

Action Steps: Rehearse for the X

1. Reflect and write out your dirt dive or pre-event routine. Before certain events pan out, how will you prepare in a way that is both thorough and confidence inspiring?
2. For at least one X moment, write out a performance statement that contains confidence-inspiring language and performance cues. Test this statement out during rehearsal.

CHAPTER 12

CONTINGENCIES

"Everyone has a plan until they get punched in the mouth." This famous Mike Tyson quote was a favorite one for my Warrior Toughness psychologist teammates.

In almost any high-stakes or important moment it is essential to have a thorough plan. We need to have the objective in mind and gear our preparation toward getting the most optimal end state. As with any combat operation, your plan should contain the appropriate contingency planning. You may be tasked to head up a training meeting or host a series of clients or partners at an event. In that case, the contingencies might involve various transportation hiccups, or maybe one or more of the vendors falls through. You must have a trained response rather than a flailing reaction.

WHEN IT ALL GOES WRONG

The phone rang in my dusty office in western Iraq. On the other end of the line was a representative of a government agency who often provided us with high-value enemy targets to pursue.

"Hey, we've got something for you. We had some targets that popped not far from you guys. Can you action it for us tonight?"

"Sure," I said. "We have no plans."

We pulled up the coordinates and got the guys moving and putting together a tactical plan. I was the senior-enlisted leader for an eighteen-man SEAL platoon. As chief petty officer, I reported directly to the platoon commander. It was my job to run the training and tactics of the platoon and oversee tactical maneuver elements on a combat operation.

This was a TST, or time-sensitive target, meaning it called for a hasty but thorough plan to grab these guys before they disappeared again. For this operation we would depart our airfield on four Black Hawk helicopters and land several kilometers outside the target village and sneak in on foot.

The flight would take around thirty minutes. It was wintertime and riding in the door of the Black Hawk made for a cold ride. The thin Mechanix work gloves that I wore gave little warmth and I could only hope that we didn't get in a gunfight upon insert, at least until my hands had a chance to warm up and had enough feeling to work my weapons system. While I sat there, I went over in my mind the plan again and spent time thinking through the remaining phases of the operation and what each of the contingencies was if things went off script and we were thrown a curveball.

The landing and patrol into the objective went without incident as the snipers and point element, or recce team, as we called them (for *reconnaissance*), led us to the target compound, a series of small buildings. The team closed on the primary target building looking like green-eyed ghosts from the faint reflection of their night vision goggles. The recce team would surround the building, peering in the windows with infrared lasers and floodlights looking for threats. All quiet. The assault team prepared to make a quiet entry, and the four team leaders in the platoon checked in with me when their teams were ready. All radio communication sequences were passed at a whisper so as not to wake anyone on the inside.

"Charlie Zero-Two, this is Charlie One-Six, commencing silent breach."

"Roger," I responded.

Before I even dropped my hand from the radio switch, a voice on the radio shouted, "Avalanche! Avalanche!" (This is not the actual code word.)

We all knew instantly what this meant. The entry team had spotted something that could be a house-borne explosive device, which could mean a trap. In seconds, the building could blow up. We dropped everything and ran, getting as much distance as we could between us and the building as quickly as possible.

We also knew that if the enemy didn't blow us up, they would likely engage us with small-arms fire. Our heads were on a swivel as we scanned the terrain with our infrared lasers and flashlights, looking for threats.

As the tactical leader of the platoon, I scanned for threats like everyone else but quickly came off my gun, knowing that I had the responsibility to make the call as to what to do next. The leader's job is to read the situation and think ahead while the operators, or sled dogs, as we say, are dealing with the immediate problem.

The guys were waiting for this. I scanned the terrain and spotted a berm that would make good cover for us to set up a hasty defensive posture. I put out a quick directive on the radio. The SEAL operators in this platoon were a highly talented and professional group that needed minimal direction to get into position and be ready to fight.

Again, as a leader I had to think about what was next. We had not been shot at, but we were unorganized and mixed up. We needed a good head count and to get everyone back into their original elements, or teams. A brief call from me over the radio for team reconsolidation and head count was all that was needed for the team leaders to make it happen.

As all of this was happening, it wasn't lost on any of us that although we were not going into that building at that moment, we were here to grab guys and that objective hadn't changed . . . yet, at least.

When the "Avalanche" call came out, there was a trained response rather than a flailing reaction. We had considered the possibility of a house-borne explosive device and had rehearsed that contingency. As a result, the operators moved swiftly and decisively. If you are thorough in your contingency planning and rehearsal, you will move swiftly through any challenge that you prepared for.

TRAINING FOR CONTINGENCIES: REHEARSED RESPONSE VERSUS REACTION

In the military, we develop our contingencies for every phase of the operation. Doing this allows it to be chunked down and organized, but more importantly, the contingency often influences or completely changes the next phase of the operation, like a domino effect. The first phase of the operation starts before you even launch on a combat mission. If, for example, we are doing a helicopter assault and have planned to use four helicopters, but suddenly one is unable to fly, we may have to execute our first contingency. When this happens, we consult our bump plan, which determines what is the minimum force required to execute the operation. We would take some of the key players off the one broken helo and disperse them onto the other helos. If another helo breaks, then we are likely unable to execute the mission. The next phases may address a downed helo due to mechanical issues or enemy fire. If we land successfully and are moving to our objective but get compromised by the enemy and therefore lose the element of surprise, we have a plan for that too.

Not every event or situation requires such planning, but if there is any degree of complexity or there are moving pieces, then I highly suggest you break it down into phases and walk or talk your way through it.

Rehearsal of Contingencies

Considering your contingencies is a good first step, but without rehearsal, you are still likely to be back on your heels when faced with that contingency. You will be more reactive instead of truly able to respond decisively.

Once contingencies and the plans to address them have been identified, then you must put the work in and prepare as appropriate. This is especially important when it comes to the actions on the X themselves.

1. Take the time to rehearse your response to the various curveballs you may get thrown from the client or leadership suite.

2. Talk to your team. You might need to socialize what the best answer is first.

3. Nail down your response and literally practice it. Get a coworker to watch you walk through it. When you are well versed on the what-ifs, you will feel even more confident going into your engagement.

The No-Contingency Contingency

We do our best as professionals to ensure that we address any possible curveballs or unplanned scenarios. We do our very best to address reasonable possibilities, but sometimes we won't have the exact answer when life goes off script. In these moments we must again think about response versus reaction. Being reactive means that you do whatever instinctively pops into your mind. If you are an athlete, such as a basketball or baseball player, and someone randomly throws a ball at your face, you will likely respond in a certain way rather than reacting like someone who has never played sports. When you are thrown curveballs in a professional setting, such as a presentation, or even on a family vacation, your ability to respond is much greater if you have spent some time developing the what-if mindset. The more time you spend thinking about and rehearsing contingencies, the more poise you will have when a scenario for which you have not trained presents itself.

Action Steps: Rehearsing Response Versus Reaction to Practice for Contingencies

1. Using one of your "On the X" events or engagements, identify any potential obstacle or potential off-script moment. Write out your answer or response to these curveballs.

2. Determine which contingencies need mental rehearsal and which ones need a thorough walk-through and actual rehearsal.

3. Add to your performance statement the phrasing that acknowledges your ability to maintain poise and focus in the event of any unplanned or unexpected contingencies.

CHAPTER 13

SITUATIONAL AWARENESS

The traffic finally started to ease as Nicole was nearing her destination. She had jumped in her car earlier that morning to make the three-hour drive down to see the doctor she had been waiting to see for months. Dr. Suvian was a highly respected nephrologist and known as a thought leader in the nephrology community.

As a specialty pharmaceutical sales representative, Nicole was in the elite segment of the pharma sales industry, responsible for knowing disease state and clinical data inside and out. She had been a drug rep for nearly twenty years with experience working for more than a half-dozen different companies. No matter what drug or company, Nicole had demonstrated consistently that she was a top performer. She was always at the top in any organization that she was a part of. What did Nicole know and do that enabled her success and consistently set her apart from her peers?

In her mind she was going through the game plan. She had an agenda and knew exactly what Dr. Suvian needed to hear. Part of Nicole's game plan included discussing new clinical data from a recent medical journal and patients who may be potential candidates for her drug. She also wanted to convince him to attend one of her upcoming dinner programs that she was hosting. All of this, and of course she was going to convince him to prescribe her drug.

Nicole arrived at the medical building and checked in with the office manager up front. After a brief wait, the manager led Nicole back to the doctor's office. Nicole was about to walk into the office when she paused. Outside in the hallway were patients lined up, waiting to see him—more than she was accustomed to seeing. She walked in and the two exchanged greetings. She could see papers and folders piled up on his desk and that he was clearly overwhelmed. She was ready to execute the game plan and launch on her agenda when she stopped herself.

She looked at Dr. Suvian and said, "I see now is not a good time. I am going to come back another time."

The doctor, seemingly aware of how important the meeting was for Nicole, said, "Wait, we can do this. I know you drove all this way."

Nicole said, "No, those patients out there are your priority, so we can reschedule for another time." With that she left and drove the three hours back home.

She drove all that way for nothing, right? Five hours later Nicole's cell phone rang and it was Dr. Suvian. "Nicole, I really appreciate the awareness that you showed. Thank you for letting me deal with the patients—it really was a hectic time. If you have time next Tuesday, I would like you to come back down. I think I may have some patients for you. Oh, and that dinner program next month: count me in."

So often we barge into a situation, ready to vomit forth our agenda. We know what we want to say, what that customer or team needs to hear. We know exactly how things should go . . . and we end up missing some very vital information because we don't stop. We don't listen or we don't hear and see what the environment is telling us.

DEVELOPING SITUATIONAL AWARENESS: ARE THEY PICKING UP WHAT YOU ARE PUTTING DOWN?

When we are on the X, it is easy to have tunnel vision, or as we say in Teams, to be too front-sight focused. When engaged in a firefight, every SEAL operator feels the urge to run the enemy down and engage them. The operators will return fire and take appropriate action, but as professionals, they know that they must pause, read the situation and the terrain, and make a thoughtful and deliberate decision before jumping in with both feet. How can we use the terrain for our tactical advantage? How are the men fixed on ammunition? Do we have good security coverage in all directions to ensure that the enemy is not maneuvering up in our blind spots?

In situations where our energy or arousal is up, it is easy to get carried away or fixated on a very narrow view of things in front of you. Whether it's from nervousness or excitement, we can often lose our situational awareness or self-awareness. We are so focused on our agenda and getting things out that we can fail to see what is unfolding in front of us or how our words or actions are affecting others. Prior to and throughout important engagements with others, remind yourself to stop, take a beat, and assess the situation. Are your talking points landing? Are those you're engaged with picking up what you're putting down and tracking what you're saying?

VARIABLE FOCUS

In my earlier "Avalanche" story, I mentioned the need for the tactical leader on the battlefield to scan for and engage threats in front of them while ensuring that they come off the gun to look around and assess. When the pressure is on, you must have the ability to toggle between the micro and the macro view. In a situation that needs focus and concentration, such as complicated sequences or detailed product offerings, you must talk yourself through the steps to ensure you apply that laser-like focus when need be. You are applying high levels of focus to the micro view of what is in front of you, but equally as important is your ability to stop and zoom out for the macro view that gains you the overall situational picture.

Another great example of this is the first responder or doctor on scene for a mass casualty event such as a terrorist bombing or train crash. The doctor is likely to be very fearful of their own safety, but they have to take in the entire picture and ensure victims are being triaged properly. Once the doctor commits to work on a particular patient, then they must apply micro focus to lifesaving medical procedures. At some point, when possible, they may look up and continue to assess the scene and give direction before diving back into the treatment.

SELF-AWARENESS CHECK AND REFRAMING YOUR THOUGHTS

In case you haven't noticed it yet, self-talk is very important in general but is critical to performing on the X. In the "Mental Skills" chapter and in the section on performance statements, I discussed how powerful our thoughts are in shaping and influencing our behaviors, emotions, and ultimately our performance. If we are reactive and don't manage the talk in our minds, then we are often sabotaged by negative or destructive thoughts.

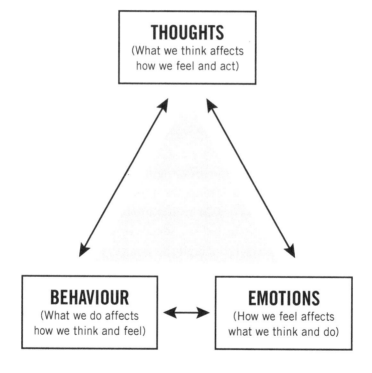

The cognitive triangle is a key component of cognitive behavioral therapy and shows the relationship between our thoughts, feelings, and behaviors. It is essential that we understand the importance of framing our internal dialogue with thoughts that positively influence our feelings and behaviors.

Renowned celebrity psychologist Dr. Elizabeth Lombardo coaches celebrities, athletes, business leaders, and adolescents alike. One essential practice that she teaches them all is to listen better to their inner world—be conscious of the thoughts in their minds. She teaches her clients to log their negative thoughts and to come up with helpful ones that replace the self-sabotaging ones. In situations where her clients are prone to feel distress, she trains them to check their thoughts. When an emotion such as fear or anger is strong enough, it is easy to become hijacked by the emotion and get swept away, or put into the red zone, as she calls it. The red zone is where we lose emotional control; we are in the fight, flight, or freeze mode.

When you know ahead of time the situations that may cause you distress or knock you off your game, you can build in the habit to constantly check your thoughts to ensure you are following your performance statement or your directed self-talk script. When you observe negative thoughts, you instantly reframe and replace them with the positive thoughts that you have at the ready.

If, for example, you find yourself stumbling during a presentation or proposal, you might notice thoughts such as "I'm an idiot, and everyone thinks I suck." Because you know that mistakes happen, you are programmed to check your thoughts the second things go off script. You catch yourself, and immediately replace those thoughts with something such as "Everyone knows that mistakes happen, but I will recover, and how I finish is what matters!" There is often a fine line between certain emotions, and sometimes the sensations are very similar; this can be helpful in how we reframe our thoughts. The sensations of fear and excitement can be similar. Think about how you may have felt when riding a roller coaster as a kid. There may have been some fear in anticipation, but there was probably exhilaration as well, especially when the ride was over. When Olympic swimmer Dana Vollmer noticed thoughts of fear or nerves before a competition, she would reframe and redirect by acknowledging the emotion. "I'm nervous. Good! This is important, I *get* to do this thing that I love." A simple reframing of our negative thoughts can do wonders for our confidence and performance.

Action Steps: Practicing Situational Awareness

1. For your upcoming high-stakes engagement, identify what areas will require high degrees of concentration or micro focus and what areas require more of a macro or balcony view of the overall situation. Plan how you are going to navigate between the two.

2. In your high-stakes moments, list any negative thoughts that you are likely to have. How will you rehearse and create cues or self-talk phrasing that will keep you on track?

CHAPTER 14

AGILITY

There is a popular expression in the SEAL Teams: "Slow is smooth, smooth is fast." That simply means that well-practiced and consistent movements and procedures will generate more speed and precision than rushed and often jerky or sloppy movements that result from an intense focus on speed.

The prior "Avalanche" story is a great military example of agility and flexibility. The platoon's swift response was made possible largely by being brilliant on the basics and our thorough rehearsal of contingencies. We had a plan to respond to a possible house-borne explosive device and we took decisive action very quickly. As I discussed before, you will not always be able to fall back on a specific contingency sequence, but your ability to be agile, adaptable, and flexible often determines your effectiveness and success in a high-stakes moment.

You have put in the work to become brilliant on the basics. You have developed mental skills to manage your internal experience. You have planned and rehearsed your actions and developed your contingency plans, or what-ifs. You have made it a priority and routine to pause and read the environment and situation. Now things come together, and you can roll with the heavy waves and stay focused and engaged. Here are a few highly effective military tools that can help organize your thoughts and actions to be more agile.

PLANNING FOR AGILITY, PART 1: THE OODA LOOP

In the early 1950s, an air force colonel named John Boyd developed the OODA loop as a way for fighter pilots to gain the tactical advantage over their adversaries in aerial combat. OODA stands for observe, orient, decide, and act. The philosophy behind the loop, or cycle, maintained that the pilot who could respond the quickest with sound decisions in the face of a rapidly changing environment would be the victor. Decisions are made in this linear fashion.

Observe. This is simply reviewing all incoming data. Decisions are not made at this point, but relevant information is separated from anything irrelevant as one attempts to grasp the full picture of what is happening.

Orient. At this point, the new information is being analyzed. The incoming information is blended with current tactics, practices, and past experiences.

Decide. With the understanding of the latest data, or information, a decision or hypothesis of the best course of action is made.

Act. Beyond simply taking action at this point, assessments of the action taken and the results are measured. At this point the iteration through the loop starts again with more current and accurate information to observe and process.

To be clear, this is a very oversimplified explanation of what is a very well-thought-out and philosophically deep model. Today, this model is used mostly as a way to make rapid decisions in a combat or competitive business situation. The focus is almost always on speed, which I believe sells the model short. Rather than thinking of this model as something used for rapidly outflanking an opponent, let's think of it as a tool for solid and deliberate decision-making in ambiguous, uncertain, or downright stressful situations.

Anthony Trucks: Performing on the X with Systemic Agility

Today Anthony Trucks is a speaker, identity coach, and author, but he began his career on the football field playing Division I college football and then spent years in the NFL. His second act was born of a commitment to being his best self and using his mission statement as his guide. As a result, he was able to refine what was important in his life, and he manifested that mission statement by preparing and using the OODA loop philosophy to be agile and ultimately successful in his prolific career beyond football.

As a professional speaker, Anthony uses what he learned on the football field to prepare and execute when the stakes are high. One day, he found himself as one of the final candidates to present for a giant telecom company. Landing this corporate speaking gig would put him on the map as a much higher-level speaker in the professional space; if selected, he would be one of three speakers who would fly to corporate headquarters and perform for both a live in-person audience and more than twenty thousand employees watching remotely via livestreaming.

Part of the final selection process required him to virtually present a sample of his speech from his home studio to the corporate leaders and meeting planners. Just as it was his turn to present, suddenly the tech side of his presentation went to pieces. His opening videos were glitching and his slides didn't appear on the program the company was using to view them.

"In this moment I had two choices. A, I could ask for five minutes to problem-solve or ask to reschedule, or B, I could pivot and deliver in the face of this challenge. I chose B and drove through and delivered. I'm a pro and can still rock this! It was my opportunity to show the event planners that if I can deliver a great product in the face of challenge, imagine what I can do when everything is working well." Anthony was selected for the event and went on to knock it out of the park for the client.

PLANNING FOR AGILITY, PART 2: THE FIVE-PARAGRAPH PATROL ORDER

The five-paragraph patrol order, or field order, is a basic framework used by the US and other militaries around the world to put together a tactical plan. It is also referred to by its acronym, SMEAC. Though this was often used as a thorough and deliberate planning and briefing format, we also use it in the field when faced with hasty taskings or when changes to the original plan are needed. When you are faced with a contingency or elements of confusion when the plan goes awry, work yourself through this basic framework to evaluate and get organized to proceed.

1. **Situation.** This refers to the enemy or friendly forces' disposition and other factors relating to an operation. What is the situation that you are currently facing with respect to obstacles and challenges? What capabilities and limitations do you have for meeting these?
2. **Mission.** With a desired end state or outcome in mind, how will you achieve it? It can be stated as "I/we will do X in order to achieve Y." For example, to overcome a customer's objections about your product or service, your mission will be to demonstrate ease of use in order to address their fears.
3. **Execution.** With the end in mind, figure out the specifics of how you are going to accomplish your mission. What are the key tasks and assignments for you or for those on the team? Contingencies should be discussed here as well.
4. **Administration/logistics.** What details must be taken care of in the form of technical support, transportation, and other logistics? Don't risk mission failure by not sewing up the small yet essential details.
5. **Communications.** What plans and steps need to be communicated with the team or client? How will this be done effectively? Sometimes it works just to slow things down and calmly talk through the basic steps and requirements for success, just like a checklist.

CREATING AGILITY IN YOUR LIFE

It can be difficult to apply these practices to your life—some of these examples feel extreme. But performing *on the X* is whatever you define as your *high-stakes moments*. Here is an example of a family trip (a high-stakes moment for my family!) where I created space and opportunity to be agile.

Situation: My family and I really need a vacation to recharge, reconnect, and create positive memories.

Mission: Conduct a five-day visit at Disney's Magic Kingdom and surrounding theme parks.

Execution: Lay out scheme of maneuver for all legs of the ground and air travel plan. Detailed itinerary for each day. Backup plans are made for flight delays and weather issues on the ground. Because it's a vacation, the itinerary is not set in stone and can be changed for something better or to just relax and do nothing.

Administration/logistics: Besides being present with your loved ones, the logistics are usually the primary element of focus when it comes to making a vacation a low-stress and successful event. Here's some logistics planning:

- Gear/clothing list
- IDs, pre-check info, passports, etc.
- Assignments: who is responsible for each piece of luggage, etc.
- Itineraries, confirmations, tickets organized

Communications: Might not be a huge factor for a vacation, but ensure confirmation on all reservations: airlines, airport transport, rental car, event tickets, and lodging. Brief every family member (age appropriately) on what their role is and how they can do their part to ensure a fun and smooth vacation. Brief plans for meeting back up in the event of separation at various venues and locations. What happens if someone is separated from the group and loses their phone?

DON'T GET HANDCUFFED

"No plan survives first contact with the enemy." The takeaway here is not that planning is unnecessary—it absolutely is. The plan is the superhighway that get us where we need to go, but agility is knowing what exit to hop off on when there is trouble ahead. As we say in the Teams, "Plan your dive, and dive your plan" until no longer feasible or sensible. All the things that you have learned up to this point make agility possible. Your commitment drives you to do what it takes to be your best. The mental skills will lower your arousal energy and enable you to think critically under pressure. Rehearsal and contingency planning allow you to be well prepared and ready for that curveball. Frameworks like SMEAC and the OODA loop help you organize and streamline thoughts and actions to serve up a hasty but useful plan when required. Stick to your plan or agenda, but don't be handcuffed by it when a better option presents itself. Plan to be agile!

Action Steps: Creating Agility

1. Write out your plan for the next major professional event or family vacation.
2. Now write down three areas that may offer you an opportunity or require you to be flexible, to pivot and adjust. Identify areas or moments where you will have to be light on your feet. What information do you need to be looking for in order to pivot? What obstacles may present themselves, and how will you respond versus react?

Part 4

COMMIT

REFLECT X PREPARE

EXECUTE

It would be unfair and naive of me to simply say a specific type of reflection works for the military, so everyone else should do it like the military does. But regardless of how you measure performance, you must employ a system and process of review. Sometimes that process is literally as simple as reflecting on what we did well and what we can improve on or do more of. In other cases, when we are really looking to be better in certain areas or maintain a positive improvement trajectory, a more deliberate and focused approach is required. In any case, it's important to manage feedback to generate actionable insights, recognize opportunities to improve, and separate the execution from the intended outcome.

MLB all-star Michael Cuddyer credits his ability to effectively reflect and detach from some of his experiences with being able to positively respond to challenging situations and circumstances. "Though I didn't officially discover Stoicism during my career, as I have learned more about it, I realize that I had been using Stoicism all along when responding to adversity. When I faced setbacks, whether it was related to performance or injury, I never really looked at it as adversity at all. It was just what happened, and it is what I have to go and deal with. It was never 'Oh God, I have another injury,' or 'Oh no, I'm in another slump.' It was simply 'I'm hurt, and I have to get better.' Or 'I'm in a slump, and I have to figure it out.' This philosophy also helped to keep me grounded when I met with success."

In this final section of the book I share with you a process to review your performance, how to manage reactions when giving and receiving feedback, the mindset to view every outcome as an opportunity, and the understanding that if you work the WTP system to deliver your best performance, even when the outcome is suboptimal, you have much to be proud of.

CHAPTER 15

AFTER-ACTION REVIEW AND ASSESS

"Drummy, if you had just given me five more minutes, I would have finished the clearance and we would have gotten that guy!" Brad, one of my team leaders, was irritated that I had pulled him and his team off their tactical objective of clearing a two-story structure in search of a high-value target (HVT). I had made the decision to pull him off in favor of reconsolidating our assault force to go after another HVT that was spotted fleeing the area in a vehicle.

As it turned out, the other HVT was in fact hiding in one of the last few rooms on the second floor of Brad's building, and by pulling them, the HVT had gotten away. Brad was rightly irritated. The good news was that this was a pre-deployment training scenario. From my perspective, my working relationship with my team leaders was still in its infancy. We had not learned to trust one another yet—we were still figuring things out.

This conversation was happening in what we refer to as a "hot wash," or debrief. This process is part of the overall military after-action review process, or AAR. After full-scale exercises like this one or actual combat operations, we conduct a thorough debrief. At the end of this particular three-week urban-warfare training block, the troop leadership would collectively work on and submit an after-action report that would document the facts and recommendations for improvement to tactics, equipment, and logistics.

This hot wash was radically candid, and though it was led by key leaders and our instructor cadre, even the most junior operators had a voice and shared their perspectives. Had Brad not been heard, and had I not taken it on board, there would have been no two-way trust built and no adjustment made to refine and adjust practices and procedures. In my view, Brad and I had just worked something out in our professional relationship, and I was pleased. I told him that were we ever in a similar situation and it was for real, he would have my trust and benefit of the doubt.

Those in the military, like professional athletes, have the luxury of operating in cycles. Professional athletes have their preseason training and in-season schedule, followed by recovery and rebuilding in the off-season; military personnel have professional development and pre-deployment training phases conducted before an overseas deployment. The luxury here is an intense singular focus on learning, practicing, and refining. The business world often has no such luxury as the focus is on day-to-day production and output. Consequently, there is seldom a dedicated focus on analysis and assessment. Most people at organizations today feel that there is simply not enough time for detailed retrospectives. There are only so many hours in a workday, but ask yourself what you are giving up or leaving on the table if you don't take the time to assess, analyze, and reflect on performance and progress toward goals. This is true for a large organization, a smaller team, and especially for the individual.

LESSONS LEARNED: MILITARY-STYLE REVIEW

The process of reflecting on lessons learned is one of the top strengths of the US military. I believe there are few better examples of this than those found in the US Special Operations and Aviation communities. As we say in the SEAL Teams, our rules and lessons are written in blood. We work hard to ensure that deadly mistakes are not repeated, and our principles and procedures reflect that.

In the Teams we admire expertise in any shape or form, and if there is a process or practice that we can take, adapt, and make our own, we will eagerly do so. Though the military AAR may not translate exactly to you or your organization, it is a simple and proven process, and much of it can be adapted to your personal and professional situations.

DEBRIEF

At the wave-top levels, here is how we use the after-action review and lessons-learned process in the SEAL Teams. After shorter training runs or scenarios, you will hear "Bring it in for the debrief!" This debrief may occur after sending two operators in to clear a room in a close-quarter combat run or after a twenty- to thirty-minute land warfare run-and-gun scenario where immediate action drills and tactics are practiced. In disseminating lessons learned after a training scenario, speed and efficiency are the name of the game since we want to minimize the turnaround and get more training reps and sets in. In a larger, more drawn-out training scenario, there is much attention to the detail of individual and team actions. There is no time for delicacy or beating around the bush. Straight and to the point with little regard for the recipient's feelings. If the debrief points are not fully understood, then there will be a brief discussion, but anything beyond that will be an additional sidebar. There is usually little time because, as soon as that debrief is conducted, you are likely going to load up and do it again or move on to a more progressive scenario.

HOT WASH

A hot wash reviews every aspect of a real mission as opposed to small chunks of it as discussed above; it's the whole enchilada. Noteworthy actions of the individual operators will be discussed, though the hot wash is typically geared toward unit performance. The mission plan, the insert and extraction platforms, and methods will be discussed in addition to actions taken on the objective. The supporting asset personnel, such as aircrews and pilots, are also likely to be in attendance or will at least pass on the lessons-learned points from their perspective. As I discussed in the "Be Brilliant on the Basics" chapter, mission success or failure often hinges on some of the less glamorous details such as organization and logistics. This is discussed below in relative detail.

Hot-Washing Your Business Practices: Student Maid Case Study

Student Maid was a highly successful organization that grew from a handful of employees in 2009. As the name suggests, Student Maid recruited and trained college students to clean homes and businesses. The company relied heavily on the use of reflection and assessment at both the organizational and individual levels. Student Maid was known not only for its on-demand cleaning services but also for its employee leadership-development opportunities. Daily reflection and assessment processes are some of the essential leadership-development practices that Student Maid used to develop their employees. Student Maid leadership development was so effective that, in 2021, founder and CEO Kristen Hadeed and her team made the decision to transition from Student Maid the cleaning business to Student Made, an arm of her business that focuses on the development of young leaders.

Kristen explains how her organization effectively uses daily reflection and assessment for organizational improvement and individual professional development:

> We incorporate reflection into every meeting we have as a team. Before we end a leadership team meeting, for example, I have each person sum up how they felt about the meeting in a couple words and then rate it 1 to 10 (10 being highest) so that I have a better understanding of how I performed as a facilitator. We encourage our team members to give us feedback regularly and candidly, and at least a couple times a year, we try to have a leadership team member sit down with them individually to check in with them and ask what they think we can be doing better as a company.
>
> The best thing you can do to make sure you learn

from your mistakes is to be intentional about reflection. Make it part of your everyday life by adding it to your schedule, or add it to your meeting agendas. Keep it simple: Just ask yourself, what did I do well today? What could I have done better? Soon enough, it'll become second nature.

LESSONS LEARNED: REPORTING RESULTS THROUGH AN AFTER-ACTION REVIEW

The after-action review is frequently used by the US military and has even found its way into the business world. This feedback system incorporates the debrief and hot wash and is typically conducted after key milestone training events or larger-scale combat operations.

The AAR process conducted by larger military units is very involved and highly detailed, and beyond the scope of this writing. However, elements of the AAR can be applied to your high-stakes business moments. You can create a model for your own AAR to conduct after big events. Your AAR should include unbiased external evaluators or graders to help you evaluate your performance.

HOW TO RUN AN AFTER-ACTION REVIEW

Per US Army doctrine,[3] the AAR provides feedback for all training. Regardless of who facilitates the review, the intent is that it's a participative process that encourages a productive and candid discussion between individuals and leaders at every level of the operation. The description of the AAR process is very detailed, but when distilled and broken down, it essentially looks as follows:

1. **The plan.** What was supposed to happen? Did the unit meet the preplanned objectives of the operation? Did

---

3. *Field Manual No. 7-0: Training* (2021), Appendix K.

the exercise or activity itself meet the unit commander's intent for training in that particular area?

2. **The event.** What actually happened? This itself can be contentious as the unit's members can be defensive about performance, especially if it is perceived that things did not go well. Because of this, leadership needs to step forward and set the right tone. All participants (leadership, evaluators, opposing force role players, and unit members) need to give their version of how they saw things.

3. **The evaluation.** What went right and what went wrong? With the guidance of the evaluators, discuss what went well and what areas were weak points or require further training or exploration. This cannot be done effectively without firmly established standards on which to measure performance by.

4. **The fix.** The way ahead for corrective measures must be clear. Whether it is retraining, equipment gaps, or further discovery after the review, there should be a plan of action moving ahead.

After the review is conducted, a report is drafted. This document captures the respective lessons learned from every level of operation or leadership. The report highlights the points that inform higher levels of leadership, but it also serves as a historic document, should a unit need to reconnect with the lessons learned when returning to a certain training or location.

Without deep assessment and reflection, we are unable to implement course change or adjust to better our outcome. Unfortunately, what I often observe in the business world is an aversion to such practices due to time constraints or low prioritization, or that these practices simply lack structure and focus. As someone who spent a career in the military and has been indoctrinated with the need for constant assessment and analysis, this is of course hard for me to wrap my head around despite my recognition of the challenges and differences that face the business world.

Good organizations encourage these types of collaboration and radical candor and support them with appropriate resources. As a result, leaders are connected to the pulse of the organization at every level. Feedback from the line or in the field helps shape decisions and policy at the executive level. Good organizations leverage the strength and insight with those most connected to the situation or problem.

Action Steps: Your AAR

I want you to commit to an AAR process at the individual level as well as for whatever team or organization that you could positively influence with this practice. Commit to the consistent habit of reflection and assessment.

1. Identify the areas and situations in your professional and personal life where consistent assessment is needed or would be helpful. Identify what your methods and approach will be in conducting these AARs.
2. Identify upcoming dates, times, or intervals where you can stop and check in with an assessment or deliver or elicit feedback.
3. Build out your framework that matches each situation. Examples: the quick huddle or debrief after an important client call, the hot wash after a day of training, or the longer after-action report after a three-day conference.

For a free AAR framework, download it from my website: www.stephendrum.com.

CHAPTER 16

MANAGE FEEDBACK

Feedback and assessment ultimately serve two purposes: accountability and performance improvement.

In the military and especially in the SEAL Teams, debriefs and AARs are thorough and conducted with brutal candor. Regardless of your rank or title, if you make a mistake, it will get called out and discussed. This creates a culture of accountability and ensures that the feedback is focused on growth. As leaders we must demonstrate that we are accountable and that we are open to criticism.

The path to growth, improvement, and unlocking potential lies in the use of effective feedback.[4] Though many point to younger generations as craving more feedback, the research says that *all* generations value feedback, even if it is negative. Our ability to leverage the value of our experiences and take deliberate actions and steps to improve our performance is one of the biggest difference makers in reaching our goals. The feedback we receive from our managers, or that we process

---

4. Jack Zenger and Joseph Folkman, "Your Employees Want the Negative Feedback You Hate to Give," *Harvard Business Review*, January 15, 2014, https://hbr.org/2014/01/your-employees-want-the-negative-feedback-you-hate-to-give.

and give ourselves, can either drive improvement or actually hold us back by derailing progress.

FEEDBACK: NO MERCY

The Black Hawk helicopter I was riding in touched down on a dark and dusty strip in the hot desert night. I hopped out, and with the other SEAL operators in several helicopters, we loaded up in vans that would take us back to the staging area, where we would conduct a hot wash of the operation.

We had just conducted a nighttime raid on a village in the middle of the desert in a remote training area in the western United States. The raid was part of a larger weeklong exercise that was part of our pre-deployment training. There were whole villages complete with Arab-speaking role players. Painstaking efforts were made to replicate the remote areas of Iraq where our unit would be deploying to in less than two months.

It was a graded exercise, and I was the tactical leader. Things had not gone well. More importantly, I was looking at it as one last opportunity to work on some new tactics that I wanted to use against the enemy when we deployed in Iraq.

When the helos touched down to insert us into the training exercise in the middle of the night, we patrolled our way to the objective, very much anticipating a sleeping or darkened village . . . at least that was the likely scenario we had planned for. As we closed on the target, we quickly realized that instead of the dark village with maybe a few streetlights, the whole town was lit up with floodlights. What we discovered later was that it was artificially lit up so that some VIPs could watch the operation unfold from a nearby rooftop.

Now, instead of employing the new tactics that required darkness, we were stuck in some dog and pony show. I was livid!

We ultimately succeeded in our mission, but many mistakes were made. As the tactical leader of the situation, I was responsible.

When we all gathered at the staging area for the debrief, the officer in charge of running the training immediately set in on us. "Back when I was in Iraq," he said, "we did this . . . If I was running this operation, I would have done this . . ."

I felt that much of his criticism was unfair, and it did not sit well with me. I am not someone who is known for being able to hide my emotions at all times, so I am sure he could see that I was not receptive to what he was putting out.

I was not immediately receptive to the feedback that was given by the training officer. I was defensive. I questioned not only the relevance of his feedback but also his credibility and if he was even the right guy to give us feedback in the first place. In short, I was not effectively processing his feedback and my negative demeanor was obvious, not only to the instructor staff but also to my guys. This is not a good look for a leader.

Unfortunately, he was not the only one who could probably read me. The rest of the guys could most likely tell that I was not picking up what he was putting down. For a leader of young warfighters, this was not the best message to send. If I expect those who work for me to take feedback on board, then I have to model that behavior as well.

As I walked back to the barracks room I was staying in, I realized that I had to put aside the embarrassment and frustration. I thought about the critique points that the officer had brought up and still believed much of the criticism was wrong or unwarranted. If I was being honest or objective, however, I knew that within those debrief points, there was information that I could learn from. There was information that I could put to use in modifying some of the tactics related to conducting night operations in varying light conditions.

ACCEPTING FEEDBACK: THREE STEPS

When it comes to processing feedback, the most important elements are humility, discipline, and commitment to improve. You must have the right mindset that actively looks for the value of the feedback and experience rather than getting waylaid by poor feedback delivery or hurt feelings.

As in the case of the post-mission hot wash in the previous story, we often have to sit and listen to feedback given to us. It is your duty, however, to take an active role in managing feedback by asking good follow-up questions and asking yourself how to use the information. When feedback is given by bosses, you may not have much latitude in directing the interaction, but you can choose to seek out specific feedback from that manager on another occasion or from someone else you trust for useful feedback.

When it comes to the feedback that we receive, process, and internalize, we are often our own worst enemy; we allow obstacles to block our path to improvement. Perhaps we allow negative prior experience or negative self-talk to get in our way. Maybe we characterize a failure or poor performance as evidence that we suck and are not good enough. Past experiences can distort how we look at our personal assessment. Why would any future attempts turn out any better? Just like I mentioned in the "Mental Skills" chapter and "Execute" part, you must check your thoughts and reframe the situation to direct the internal dialogue with thoughts that serve.

Regardless of whether things went well or poorly, process personal feedback with these three steps:

1. **Be accountable.** Regardless of the circumstances or who is to blame for failure, acknowledge your role and what you could stand to improve on. The same goes for looking for improvement on success.

2. **Practice self-compassion.** Today's climate can often seem like an unforgiving place. People may hold a grudge or be unwilling to make amends when we fall short. We don't control others' feelings and actions, so we have no choice but to forgive ourselves and move forward. I remember hearing the story of one college baseball team that kept a miniature toilet in the clubhouse. After every game, each player would go through the ritual of acknowledging mistakes and then flushing those mistakes down the toilet, never to revisit the mistakes again. Understand that you are human and will make mistakes, but flush those mistakes away to avoid having them as baggage that weighs you down moving forward.

3.   **Look ahead.** After accountability and forgiveness, reframe all that feedback into the specific steps that you are *going* to do next time. Everything is framed as positive planning for the next opportunity to perform on the X.

GIVING FEEDBACK: THREE STEPS

Do you remember what we discussed in the "Situational Awareness" chapter? Delivering feedback is a good time to summon that skill; you must pay attention to how your feedback is landing with the recipient. A study led by Dr. Jackie Gnepp provides insight into some of the impediments and barriers to performance improvement through feedback.[5] When a manager gives performance feedback that is critical in nature, the recipient often becomes defensive. As a result of self-protection and self-enhancement, the recipient often misremembers their role in something that went poorly or blames the outcome on something or someone else. Your job is to deliver feedback that enhances and improves team and company performance on the X.

To deliver feedback that's productive, focus on the following:

1.   **Make it succinct.** No one wants to be in a feedback session that goes on and on. Be empathetic and tactful, but get to the important points succinctly and directly or they will lose their punch and get lost in the noise. Highlight the most important ideas that also provide the greatest opportunity for improvement and then move on.
2.   **Make it future-focused.** The future holds optimism, and it is easier for the recipient to get on board that train. We need to be candid with the prior events, but shortfalls and corrections should be framed in the context of what can be done moving forward.

---

5.   Jackie Gnepp et al., "The Future of Feedback: Motivating Performance Improvement Through Future-Focused Feedback," *PLOS One*, June 19, 2020, https://journals.plos.org/plosone/article?id=10.1371/journal.pone .0234444.

3. **Make it actionable.** Lamenting past mistakes and "should haves" doesn't help anyone. Feedback is only useful if the recipient has a clear understanding of what they need to do next time, including continuing to do what they are already doing well.

When things go wrong, we cannot afford to ignore or sweep things under the rug. Often uncomfortable conversations do need to be had. With that, based on what the research tells us about negative feedback, we know we have to be very conscientious about how we deliver and focus our feedback.

Think about quickly pivoting to the future. While the past may hold failure or regret, the future holds optimism. Whatever went wrong in the past, take the opportunity to turn mistakes made in the past into goals and focus points for future performance.

Action Steps: Incorporating Feedback into Your Performance on the X

1. Identify a moment when you gave feedback and it was not well received. How could you have used situational awareness to identify the disconnect? How could you have delivered the feedback in a positive way?
2. Identify some specific areas where you can request feedback (i.e., communication, listening, etc.). Can you think of good follow-up questions and how to use the information you received?
3. If you are experiencing negative self-talk, reframe your failure feedback to thoughts such as "I fell short, but I learned. I am not yet where I want to be but am getting closer to my goals. Based on what I just learned, this is the adjustment I am going to make."

CHAPTER 17

OPPORTUNITY: A MINDSET

I retired from the US Navy in December 2019. By February 2020 my speaking career was starting to take off. I had been working hard to develop my content and the craft of speaking. When COVID-19 hit during March, the speaking business was almost completely shut down. Those of my peers who had been doing it for quite a while seemed to pivot to virtual speaking with relative ease. I did not. In a period of weakness, I lamented the fact that my income had dried up as I found myself tearing up advance checks to canceled speaking gigs.

One of my positive attributes is the ability to put some cognitive distance between the situation, my thoughts about it, and how it fits into the big picture. That is to say that, after some reflection, I am able to reframe negative thoughts and focus on what is really important. I have my family and am in good health. Financially, we would be OK, and I could still find a way to deliver content that I believed in, even if it meant doing it through the different medium of virtual presentations.

There have been times in my life when I have allowed myself to react poorly and fixate on things over which I had no control. I allowed circumstances, such as canceled or delayed flights, or the actions or behaviors of others, to negatively affect my actions and behaviors.

A FRAMEWORK FOR OPPORTUNITIES:
IT'S NEITHER GOOD NOR BAD

Stoicism is an ancient Greek philosophy that espouses living in accordance with cardinal virtues and in harmony with nature. Stoics valued wisdom, virtue, and character above all else.[6]

The Stoic philosophy emphasizes that one should look at circumstances and situations not as good or bad, but as opportunities to demonstrate the cardinal virtues of courage, wisdom, justice, and temperance, or moderation. While much of what happens to us we cannot control, we do control how we respond to these situations. Our response is what we need to focus on. When we begin to see every situation as holding opportunity for us, it is easier for us to avoid applying negative or unhelpful judgment to the situation, and we are better able to focus on the thoughts that serve us. This is also consistent with the practices of rational emotive behavior therapy. This form of psychotherapy helps the patient to identify unhealthy and irrational thoughts that can lead to anxiety and destructive behaviors. When the patient notices these thoughts, they are to immediately replace them with more productive and helpful ones. It's not good or bad—it's your judgment of the situation.

OPPORTUNITY IN ALL THINGS

To build our skills and mental muscle for performing on the X, we must be able to identify opportunities for growth.

In the final period of a youth hockey game, my sixteen-year-old son lost an edge and crashed awkwardly into the boards, breaking his hand. He was having a really good season and would now be sidelined for four to six weeks. Equally difficult for him was the fact that after his injury, he could not play guitar.

In the grand scheme of life and struggle, being unable to play

6. Authors such as Ryan Holiday and Donald Robertson have written extensively on Stoicism, and have also been highly effective in helping individuals and organizations adapt and adopt some of these ancient principles to great effect.

hockey for a month is inconsequential. Nevertheless, I'm proud that I taught him to see the opportunity in the situation. Finding the opportunity is not always some feel-good story about getting fired from a job and then jumping into your dream job. Sometimes it is about demonstrating strength of character. In the case of my son, it was about pivoting into working out his lower body, attacking his conditioning, but most of all, simply focusing on the things he could control. There is always opportunity for us to take ownership in responding to challenging and difficult situations, no matter the circumstances.

HOW TO IDENTIFY OPPORTUNITY

You must be able to separate the things you cannot control from the things that you can. Look back and try to remember all the times that you wrung your hands in frustration about things in which you had no control. How did that serve you? How much time and energy did you waste on that?

Develop the habit of separating the judgment from things that happen and circumstances you may find yourself in. Simply ask yourself: What is the opportunity?

I love watching professional ice hockey and am always interested in the goalies, in terms of the psychology of dealing with getting scored on. Goalies, like most professional athletes with sports psychology training, typically have a mistake ritual, or a "getting scored on" ritual. I say "getting scored on" ritual because often, as a goalie in most sports, they are placed in a situation where it is not reasonable to expect that they could have prevented the goal.

After getting scored on, you may see the goalie perform some of these rituals. It may be as simple as taking a drink from a water bottle, skating toward one side of the glass, or tapping his stick on each goal post. As he is doing that, he is using that brief period in time to assess the situation. He may be thinking, "Was I in the right position—squared up to the shot? Did I mishandle the puck? Did my defenseman do his job? Or, did I realistically have little chance to save it because I was screened and couldn't see the shot?"

The goalie must quickly sift through the information to take away what is useful. There is no time to wallow on a mistake made, because he could face another shot in a matter of seconds.

When I reacted poorly to my speaking opportunities drying up early during the pandemic, I was able to pivot and move forward only when I identified the opportunity. I could not get paid to speak on stage—or at all, for that matter, early on. What I could do, though, was take the opportunity to share my content and experience with those that I felt could be helped by it.

Here are some questions you might ask yourself when you are struggling to see an opportunity in a setback:

- If you lose your job, what else can you pursue?
- If you face the loss of a loved one, who can you connect with more deeply now?
- When you face a health crisis, how can you demonstrate courage?
- When wronged by someone else, how can you demonstrate forgiveness or grace?

What I propose above is not easy for me—it won't be easy for you either. Things such as loss often come with great pain, sometimes seemingly unbearable. You must begin to program yourself that there is no other option.

No matter what happens, no matter how hard, make a habit out of identifying the opportunity that the situation provides.

Action Steps: Finding Opportunities to Grow

1. Look ahead at your next actual or potential high-stakes moment. Develop three optimal and three less-than-desirable outcomes to your high-stakes or X moment or event.
2. For all six outcomes, identify the opportunity that each provides.

CHAPTER 18

SEPARATE OUTCOME FROM EXECUTION

During one of my final military deployments I was tasked with taking a team and flying to an eastern European country to conduct exchange training with one of our foreign partner special operations forces. This unit was a valuable ally in our fight in Afghanistan. They were disciplined, highly capable, and ferocious fighters.

On the battlefield, individual soldiering skills and tactics are just one part of the equation. On a modern battlefield there is a level of complexity that comes with managing air power, other supporting assets, and deconflicting your operation area with other friendly forces. This is often referred to as combined arms. While other foreign partner special operations forces may have been very capable soldiers, they often lacked the ability to independently conduct full-spectrum special operations combat without the embedded support of US SOF personnel on the ground with them. Our goal on exchange training exercises like this one was to further build rapport and to increase the unit's capability and capacity to operate with less reliance on US support.

After two weeks of training on weapons, tactics, and mission planning, we conducted a final training exercise (FTX), as is typical at the conclusion of most military training blocks. An FTX is the culmination of all the things that were worked on in the prior weeks and are now put to the test with a realistic full-mission scenario that must be planned, executed, and assessed. In this instance, I set up the whole scenario, which involved the kill or capture of some high-value targets. I designed the scenario to be very challenging, necessitating the need for notional close air support and other specialty and higher-level leadership skills that we had worked on. The exercise would test not just skills and tactics but also the unit's leadership capability in navigating through some challenging big-picture battlefield problems and contingencies.

In the hours leading up to the mission I was excited. We had worked hard, and I felt that our partner force had a firm grasp of the skills and tactics that we had worked on those past two weeks. Sadly, the execution of the mission itself did not go well and the unit floundered in the face of all the problems that we threw at them. In objectively observing the outcome of the FTX, it was clear that it was not a success. The ideal FTX should challenge the participating units enough that they make mistakes and learn but also allow them to walk away from the exercise with a feeling of confidence . . . assuming that the unit received quality training and put the work in on their end. This exercise did not result in a confidence-inspiring finish, and I was extremely disappointed.

In order to best move forward, it was important that I separate the unsuccessful outcome from some of the areas where they actually did perform well. Most importantly, though, was that they had a clear path and focus on where to go next.

Processing both your failure and your success for the sake of improving performance requires the ability to draw out and dissect the various elements of the performance, mission, or task outcome. Did you or your team perform exactly what was intended? Were the solutions or plans adequate for the situation or problem?

ASSESS: DID I DIVE MY PLAN?

When SEALs conduct combat diving operations, they are told to dive their plan and not to start changing things on the fly when things start to feel off or not right in terms of where they are, navigation-wise. They will adjust the plan as a last resort and only when they are sure that they must. Sometimes you must pivot and adjust, but if you are so far off your plan, it becomes difficult to measure and assess. When hot-washing and debriefing a combat dive, the essential question is always asked: "Did you dive your plan?" Was the plan faulty? Did you miscalculate the tides and currents? Did you make a mistake on the compass bearings? Or, did you fail to execute a sound dive plan for whatever reason? Did you get lost under a pier or not dive at the right pace (speed)?

When we get a certain outcome, we must evaluate the factors that led to that outcome. If we were unsuccessful, we must know exactly why so we can implement the proper corrections. The same holds true for success. If we expect to repeat that success and ultimately build on it, then we must know what enabled that success. Did we dive our plan?

Professional speaking is like being in the military in that respect. Michael Port, of Heroic Public Speaking, teaches his students that when they feel their speech does not seem to connect or resonate with the audience, they must first ask themselves if they executed the speech exactly as rehearsed. It would not be useful to start changing the content of your speech if in reality the content was fine but it was poorly delivered or executed. When you fail to connect with a client or a team that you are leading, or otherwise don't successfully execute, ask yourself these three questions:

1. Did I adequately prepare, and was I equipped with the right resources and information?
2. Did I execute the plan exactly as I intended? If not, why?
3. Did I execute the wrong plan for the challenge or problem I faced?

As you can see, there are three entirely different considerations needed to address improving the outcome next time.

Performance Versus Outcome

AJ stepped off the ice and made the awkward hockey goalie shuffle back to the locker room. His team had just lost an important play-off game and he was incredibly disappointed. Some of his teammates angrily threw their sticks to the floor. Despite the loss, the coach and his teammates congratulated AJ for playing an amazing game. He had stopped thirty-seven of thirty-nine shots. He had given his team every opportunity to win. Just two weeks prior, AJ had played one of his worst games of the season. He let in two pretty soft goals and another that he felt he really should have had. His team, however, battled back to ultimately win the game. He was happy for his team but very dissatisfied with his performance. Win or lose, AJ knows that it is critical to separate what is on the scoreboard from how well he played in net.

I used the same philosophy when conducting the FTX hot wash with our foreign SOF partners. They needed to realize that though a more successful outcome in terms of meeting the mission objectives and building confidence was ideal, the value of identifying critical gaps and strengthening areas they were already proficient at was more important. Our partner force came up short, but they had done well when considering how much I had thrown at them. In some areas the unit performed exactly to standard; in other cases they had not. Additionally, while some skills and tactics were performed properly, they were not the right skill for the task or problem. It is essential that you are able to objectively separate and evaluate your performance independent of the outcome. Much of an outcome of any situation is beyond your control. Focusing too much on the outcome diverts that essential focus away from what matters most. What matters most is focusing on what you can control—your performance to the best of your abilities and what you can improve on.

Planning for Your Next High-Stakes Event

When my business slowed to a grinding halt during the COVID pandemic, I faced doubt about the future of my business and if I needed to change course and go another direction. I had to go back to the "Commit" phase of the performing on the X model and examine my values, principles, and what gave me true purpose. I realized that the obstacles and challenges that I faced were not enough to stop me from doing the work that I was passionate about, but I would have to adjust my goals, plans, and even my skills if I wanted to be given the opportunity to share my message with the world.

Part of a thorough assessment of outcome and moving forward requires an analysis of goals, plans, and training (knowledge, skills, and procedures). Determine what goals need to be adjusted, scrapped, or what new ones need to be added. What training changes need to be made to meet these goals? If your skills, knowledge, and attributes are strong, then it is worth investing the time to see what additional plans and strategies can be modified or created from scratch.

HOT-WASHING THE BUD/S O-COURSE

When things seem to be tracking well, there is often the attitude of

"If it ain't broke, don't fix it." It can be easy to put our heads down and take our foot off the gas, but then we may fall short in our planning, preparation, and execution.

When I first showed up at BUD/S, the thing that I hated most was the obstacle course, or o-course, as it was dubbed. It was all about technique and I had none. The first few times I did it, I would leave a snail trail of blood on the obstacles as the calluses on my hands were ripped off.

After a few weeks, I really started to get the hang of it. My technique improved and I began to perform better in all the other events, or evolutions. One Friday afternoon, I remember looking in the rearview mirror of my training week and thinking, "You had a great week." A great week for me at this point was one where I didn't fail any events. My confidence grew and I had the feeling that I was going to get through this training after all.

That Sunday night I got a knock on the door of my barracks room. Outside in the hall was a cast of characters, the guys that you just want to hate because of their natural abilities. They could smoke a carton of cigarettes and drink a case of beer and outperform everyone else at anything physical. They were there to convince me to go out drinking with them that night. . . . It was not a tough sell. We had a good time that night.

"Drum! Shot of tequila?"

"Sure! Make it two." I was thinking, "I got this. I'm going to get through this training and be a Navy SEAL!"

The next morning rolled around and I was hungover. The first evolution, as luck would have it, was the dreaded o-course. The third obstacle was probably the easiest of the course to navigate. It was nothing more than three or four fifteen- to twenty-foot telephone poles laid across some railroad ties. You simply had to maintain your balance as you ran across them. That morning I had a real challenge maintaining my balance and negotiating this simple obstacle.

In the SEAL Teams we always find a way to bring humor to any situation, and this starts in BUD/S. In our class we had two T-shirts that we awarded at the end of every o-course. The two awardees would wear the shirts the very next time that the class did the o-course. The first shirt was navy blue and gold and on the back it simply said, "Mr.

O-course." This was for the fastest time and was a badge of honor to wear. I was not awarded that shirt.

I got the other shirt—the one for the slowest time. This horrendous pink shirt consisted of two embroidered and sequined kittens on the front with "Miss O-course" written on the back. Political correctness is not taken too seriously in the Teams, especially back then. The shirt was an embarrassment to be seen in. It did serve an important purpose, though. You put a twenty-one-year-old alpha male in a hot-pink kitten T-shirt and it is likely to fuel him through his fastest o-course ever because he'll be damned if he is ever wearing that shirt again.

The lesson that I learned here, and thankfully learned early, is that if you take your foot off the gas, you can become complacent. When things are going well, we are performing well and have met with success, the temptation is to keep coasting along. But we also know that to optimize performance on the X, you will need a process in place that evaluates your failures and successes.

HOW TO PLAN YOUR "WHAT'S NEXT"

- **Identify and cultivate the warrior in you.** Determine your values, attributes, principles, sense of purpose, and your strength of character. Commit to this way of being through a specific and well-vetted mission statement.
- **Prepare for work and life.** Determine your objectives, short- and long-term. Put in the hard work to become brilliant on the basics and develop the mental skills that will allow you to perform in high-stakes moments. Manage your energy and mind toward achieving those objectives. Use your mission statement as your compass.
- **Execution.** When you perform on the X, rehearse, plan for contingencies, pay attention to those around you, and be agile in your actions.
- **Reflect on performance.** Review and assess. Ask for and offer productive feedback. Identify opportunity in failures and possibilities within success. Like a goalie, separate outcome from execution.

A Final Example of Performing on the X in Military and Life

John Calamos, the founder, chairman, and global chief investment officer of Calamos Investments, was a recipient of the Distinguished Flying Cross for his Vietnam service as an air force combat pilot.

John Calamos served in Vietnam as an air force forward air controller (FAC) pilot. FACs were instrumental in coordinating desperately needed air support for beleaguered US combat units. Circling the combat zone in light unarmored prop planes, they were vital in observing and coordinating fire support missions between the units on the ground and the various attack aircraft and gunships being tasked with bringing fire down on the enemy.

On September 28, 1968, two North Vietnamese Army regiments attempted to overrun a strategically vital US Army Special Forces camp near the Da Nang Air Base. As night fell, Captain Calamos climbed into his small O-2 Skymaster airplane and relieved the FAC orbiting the camp. Some of the most vital equipment on the aircraft were the ten white phosphorous rockets used to mark ground targets and three radios to separately communicate between the air base, ground unit, and attack aircraft. For four hours Calamos circled the battle, coordinating and directing fire for two sets of F-4 Phantom jets, one flare-dropping aircraft, and one AC-47 gunship. Despite poor visibility and constant enemy fire directed at his aircraft, Calamos calmly directed effective fire support that prevented the enemy from overrunning the camp and saved hundreds of Americans, Vietnamese, and Montagnard tribesmen. For his actions, President Nixon awarded Captain Calamos the Distinguished Flying Cross, one of the highest honors a US aviator can receive.

Calamos would serve a total of five years active duty and twelve years in the reserves before retiring as a major. John eventually went on to build one of the largest and most successful investment companies in the US and credits his military service for much of his success. "My military service was extremely impactful in my career in financial investments. People often ask me, 'John, how can you go from flying combat missions to going into investments?' It's exactly the same, I would say. Investing, just like flying, is about preparation and doing your homework in order to successfully manage risk. You do your homework before you take off, not after."

To optimize your life and performance on the X, implement the action steps in this book. Also, to assist you in systemizing your mission, I have created the "On the X Mission Cheat Sheet." This resource is a quick guide to ensuring you are well armed for the battle, whether it be in the field, in the boardroom, or at home. You can download this resource absolutely free on my website at stephendrum.com.

ABOUT THE AUTHOR

Stephen Drum is a retired Navy SEAL master chief petty officer with twenty-seven years of service. He served in combat in Iraq and Afghanistan and deployed on strategically vital operations around the globe. During his career, he has had the opportunity to train thousands of US and foreign special operations forces.

Drum was handpicked to become a principal architect and co-creator of the US Navy's Warrior Toughness Program, designed to provide Navy sailors and officers with the mental skills and character tools to perform under the acute pressure of combat and the stresses of military life.

Today Drum consults and coaches leaders and teams on how to perform under pressure and execute in challenging environments.

CPSIA information can be obtained
at www.ICGtesting.com
Printed in the USA
BVHW032008150223
658591BV00004B/260